James:
The Pen
and the
Plumb Line

Dr Bo Wagner

Word of His Mouth Publishers
Mooresboro, NC

All Scripture quotations are taken from the **King James Version** of the Bible.

ISBN: 978-1-941039-05-2
Printed in the United States of America
©2018 Dr. Bo Wagner
Word of His Mouth Publishers
Mooresboro, NC
www.wordofhismouth.com

Table of Contents

Introduction

As a little boy growing up in his father's carpentry shop, he became familiar with some very specific tools. One of those tools used even two thousand years ago was the plumb line. The plumb line is simply a tapered piece of metal on the end of a string. The carpenter will hold it in the air, and when it stops swinging it will give him a perfectly straight line to work with in leveling a wall. The plumb line is a very precise, unyielding thing. It will show the carpenter the perfect standard, and any deviation from that line will be seen to be in error. Little James would have learned the use of the plumb line very, very well.

Many years later, James found himself working with a completely different kind of tool-a pen. James was still living after the death of his older brother. The way his brother died made an indelible impact on him. So much so that James became a Christian and wrote the book of the New Testament that bears his name. But even while using his new tool, the pen, James found himself still using the concept of a plumb line at the exact same time. The entire book of James is a strict, straight, unyielding epistle about right and wrong. Other epistles deal much with grace and mercy; James deals much with the high expectations of holiness. Other Bible books will make you stand and rejoice. James is the counterbalance to that; it is a book that will often make you kneel and weep. James is not the most pleasant book to read, but it may just be the most necessary on a practical level. A person reading and following the book of James will be someone that no one ever mistakes for a sinner.

The lines he draws are too straight for that. One day I expect to see James on the streets of Glory. I expect that when I do, he will still be holding a pen in one hand and a plumb line in the other.

The book of James is not long numerically. It has just five chapters, and the very longest of those chapters is just twenty-seven verses. You can read the book of James in ten to twelve minutes. But though it is not a *long* book, it is a *deep* book. By that, I mean that this book, while very straightforward, is not one that you can just skim quickly along the surface if you expect to really get it. Some of the greatest minds of all times have mishandled this book and gotten into some very bad positions because of it. The most famous example of this is the leader of the Protestant Reformation, the man who nailed the *95 Theses* to the door of the castle in Wittenburg, Martin Luther. Martin Luther was a Catholic monk who got saved. After years of agonizing over the works-based religion of Rome, after years of trying everything the Catholic church teaches and yet finding no peace, Martin Luther finally turned to his Bible, and here among other things is what he found:

Romans 1:17 *For therein is the righteousness of God revealed from faith to faith: as it is written, The just shall live by faith.*

He realized that works could not save him; only faith could save him. Martin Luther got saved.

But years later, Martin Luther, brilliant, highly educated, saved Martin Luther, had these famous things to say about the book of James:

"The epistle of St. James is an epistle full of straw because it contains nothing evangelical." This was in Luther's original 1522 Preface to the New Testament, though to his credit, later editions of the work, at his insistence, omitted that phrase.

Martin Luther called James a "defective" book. (Luther) At one point he said he almost felt like throwing the book of James into the stove. He believed that *if* it was included in Scripture, it should be regarded as less authoritative than the writings of Paul and John. Martin Luther had a big problem with the book of James! If a brilliant mind like that had problems with the book of James then, believe me, we better look at it very carefully, not quickly and haphazardly. As I said it is not a *long* book, but it is a *deep* book.

A deep book that will be very much worth your while.

Chapter One
Radical Changes

James 1:1 *James, a servant of God and of the Lord Jesus Christ, to the twelve tribes which are scattered abroad, greeting.*

There is nothing quite like coming to know Christ for who He is to effect change in a life. The gospel of the resurrected Christ has changed the diet of the cannibal, the drinking habits of the drunk, the temperament of the furious man, the loose living of the prostitute, and the honesty level of everyone from paupers to presidents. If a person truly gets saved, he or she gets changed. And that change will be the first thing we come to see in the epistle of James.

Changes in the author

James 1:1 *James, a servant of God and of the Lord Jesus Christ...*

There are a few different men that carried the name James in the New Testament. There was James the son of Zebedee, the brother of John. He was killed by Herod in Acts 12 before the Jews had been widely dispersed as we find is the case in this verse. There was also James, the son of Alphaeus. There is not much evidence to support the idea that he was the writer. The third James, the one that clearly seems to be the author of this book, is the one that both Paul and the Jewish historian Josephus called the brother of Jesus. There is no reason to doubt that he is the author of this book. And that is what makes this book so very interesting right off the bat! Let us go back into the gospels for just a bit and let me show you what I mean.

Matthew 13:55 *Is not this the carpenter's son? is not his mother called Mary? and his brethren, James, and Joses, and Simon, and Judas?*

This James mentioned here, the half-brother of Jesus, is the author of the book of James. The last name on the list, Judas, is the author of the book of Jude. So, two of Jesus's half-brothers became authors of books of the New Testament. They were very clearly believers in Jesus, their half-brother. They viewed Him as being the very Son of God. But it was not always like that.

John 7:1 *After these things Jesus walked in Galilee: for he would not walk in Jewry, because the Jews sought to kill him. 2 Now the Jews' feast of tabernacles was at hand. 3 His brethren therefore said unto him, Depart hence, and go into Judaea, that thy disciples also may see the works that thou doest. 4 For there is no man that doeth any thing in secret, and he himself seeketh to be known openly. If thou do these things, shew thyself to the world. 5 For neither did his brethren believe in him. 6 Then Jesus said unto them, My time is not yet come: but your time is alway ready. 7 The world cannot hate you; but me it hateth, because I testify of it, that the works thereof are evil. 8 Go ye up unto this feast: I go not up yet unto this feast; for my time is not yet full come. 9 When he had said these words unto them, he abode still in Galilee. 10 But when his brethren were gone up, then went he also up unto the feast, not openly, but as it were in secret.*

The "after these things" mentioned in John 7:1 refers all the way back to John 5:18, where the Jews got so mad at Jesus that they decided they needed to kill Him. Six months after that, in John 7, it was the time of the Feast of Tabernacles. All Jewish males were required by law to go to Jerusalem and to live in tents around the city for seven days. But Jesus had been avoiding Jerusalem like the plague because the Jews were trying to kill Him, and it was not time for that yet. He had spent months in Galilee instead because of the Jews plotting to kill Him.

At this particular time, the time when all Jewish males were required to go to Jerusalem, Jesus was actually with His family, at least with His brothers. At some point, the discussion turned to whether or not Jesus would leave Galilee and go up to Jerusalem for the feast. Now, what would you expect brothers to advise their brother concerning a matter like that?

"Jesus, you can't go. Stay here where it is safe."

"Jesus, you need to be careful. You just lay low here, no one will know you haven't gone to Jerusalem."

"Jesus, stay here. We'll cover for you; we don't want to lose you."

That is certainly what you or I would be saying if we knew that someone wanted to kill one of our family members. (At least I hope that is what we would all be saying!)

But look at what the half-brothers of Jesus said:

John 7:3 *His brethren therefore said unto him, Depart hence, and go into Judaea, that thy disciples also may see the works that thou doest.* **4** *For there is no man that doeth any thing in secret, and he himself seeketh to be known openly. If thou do these things, shew thyself to the world.*

They were couching this in glowing terms, but it is evident what they were trying to accomplish. They were very literally trying to get their own brother killed. Look at the next verse:

John 7:5 *For neither did his brethren believe in him.*

The four half-brothers of Jesus, including James, the author of the book we are now studying, did not believe that Jesus was who He said He was. They did not believe that Jesus was who their mother Mary said He was. They thought their own brother was either a liar or a lunatic, and they were trying to get Him killed. Let that sink in; the man who wrote the New Testament book of James spent his earlier years trying to get his brother, Jesus, killed. That is one of the things that makes the opening few words of James so remarkable:

James 1:1 *James, a servant of God and of the Lord Jesus Christ...*

When the New Testament writers spoke of God and then of the Lord Jesus Christ, they were not saying that Jesus was not God. They did that as a way of distinguishing between God the Father and God the Son. But what is really of great interest to me here is that James referred to himself as the servant of both. It was nothing for a Jew to refer to himself as the servant of God, any of the Old Testament heroes would have been glad to hold that title. But for James to also refer to himself as a servant of *Jesus*, now that was remarkable.

There are two levels on which it was remarkable. On the first level, it was remarkable because James was not trading on his familial relationship to Jesus. Have you ever known people who traded on their family name or on the name of someone in their family to try and elevate themselves?

Many years ago, when we were in our original, decrepit, used-to-be-a-restaurant church building, a man showed up right after church. He did not come for the service, mind you, he carefully timed his arrival for just after service when everyone was leaving. He came looking for me, and when he found me, he introduced himself and began to tell his sad story.

He said he was the son of veteran missionaries, he told me what board his parents were with and that he had fallen on very hard times. His dad had always taught him that if you were having trouble go to God's people for help.

He said he had been looking for work left and right and could not find any. To make matters worse, his little daughter was dying down in Florida, and he desperately needed to get down to her before she passed away. Could we please, please, help him with a significant amount of money? After all, he said, his parents had given everything for the cause of Christ.

I told him we would be glad to help... as long as he had just a few minutes to wait so that I could call the mission board and verify all of this.

When I said that, he went absolutely berserk! He cursed me in language I would never dream of using and no one should hear. The few people still there were standing around with their jaws dropping open, unsure of what to do.

Once he was done cursing, he stormed out and said, "This is why everybody hates church!"

As for me, I very calmly made my way back to the office, picked up the phone, and made a call. Someone happened to be there in the office at that time, and I told them what had happened. Immediately the voice on the other end of the line said, "Oh no! Please tell me you didn't give him anything. His parents are the missionaries he told you about, and yes, they have been on the field serving faithfully all these years. But their son is a total con-artist; he doesn't even have a daughter. He has spent the last thirty years going state to state, church to church, using this con on people, and has gotten hundreds of thousands of dollars trading on his parents' good name!"

Whether it is a situation like that or a situation where someone tries to move up the social or corporate ladder by unjustly using someone else's name, it is common, but it is still wrong.

James, though, could have *accurately* opened this epistle with the words "James, a servant of God and the brother of the Lord Jesus Christ." Had he said it that way, it would have been correct and fair. Had he said it that way, it would have boosted his own reputation among the church. Had he said it that way, it would have given him a greater sense of authority.

But when James spoke of Jesus, the One that he previously tried to have killed, he in humility just referred to himself as Jesus's servant. That humility that he demonstrated is something that he would then turn and demand of others throughout the rest of this book:

James 4:6 *But he giveth more grace. Wherefore he saith, God resisteth the proud, but giveth grace unto the humble.*

James 4:10 *Humble yourselves in the sight of the Lord, and he shall lift you up.*

James 1:21 *Wherefore lay apart all filthiness and superfluity of naughtiness, and receive with meekness the engrafted word, which is able to save your souls.*

James 2:9 *But if ye have respect to persons, ye commit sin, and are convinced of the law as transgressors.*

James 3:1 *My brethren, be not many masters, knowing that we shall receive the greater condemnation.*

James 3:13 *Who is a wise man and endued with knowledge among you? let him shew out of a good conversation his works with meekness of wisdom.*

James 4:16 *But now ye rejoice in your boastings: all such rejoicing is evil.*

You get the idea from reading all of this that James had been humbled and that he expected everyone else to be humbled as well.

The second level on which this is remarkable is that James emphasized a position that was lower than what he could have claimed. Yes, he could have accurately claimed to be Jesus's brother, but he could also have accurately claimed to be much more than a servant! Look at what Paul told us that James had as a position:

Galatians 1:19 *But other of the apostles saw I none, save James the Lord's brother.*

At some point, James had become an apostle. This was the highest position in the first generation of the church. There were just a handful of these men, and in one generation, they and the office of the apostle were gone. Hundreds of thousands of people looked to them for guidance. Had James called himself an apostle of Jesus Christ, he would not have been wrong. He would also not have been sinning; even Paul called himself an apostle in almost everything he wrote. But James bypassed the usage of the term apostle and simply called himself a servant.

James had spent so much time opposing Jesus, and now he seems to have become almost just like Him. Look at this:

John 13:1 *Now before the feast of the passover, when Jesus knew that his hour was come that he should depart out of this world unto the Father, having loved his own which were in the world, he loved them unto the end. 2 And supper being ended, the devil having now put into the heart of Judas Iscariot, Simon's son, to betray him; 3 Jesus knowing that the Father had given all things into his hands, and that he was come from God, and went to God; 4 He riseth from supper, and laid aside his garments; and took a towel, and girded himself. 5 After that he poureth water into a bason, and began to wash the disciples' feet, and to wipe them with the towel wherewith he was girded. 6 Then cometh he to Simon Peter: and Peter saith unto him, Lord, dost thou wash my feet? 7 Jesus answered and said unto him, What I do thou knowest not now; but thou shalt know* *hereafter.* **8** *Peter saith unto him, Thou shalt never wash my feet. Jesus answered him, If I wash thee not, thou hast no part with me.* **9** *Simon Peter saith unto him, Lord, not my feet only, but also my hands and my head.* **10** *Jesus saith to him, He that is washed needeth not save to wash his feet, but is clean every whit: and ye are clean, but not all.* **11** *For he knew who should betray him; therefore said he, Ye are not all clean.* **12** *So after he had washed their feet, and had taken his garments, and was set down again, he said unto them, Know ye what I have done to you?* **13** *Ye call me Master and Lord: and ye say well; for so I am.* **14** *If I then, your Lord and Master, have washed your feet; ye also ought to wash one another's feet.* **15** *For I have given you an example, that ye should do as I have done to you.* **16** *Verily, verily, I say unto you, The servant is not greater than his lord; neither he that is sent greater than he that sent him.*

Jesus, the Son of God. Jesus, God the Son.

Jesus, the one that the book of Colossians tells us literally holds all things together.

This Jesus got up from the table, wrapped a towel around Himself, pulled the nasty shoes off of the filthy feet of His disciples, and one by one washed all twenty-four of those filthy, smelly, fungus-filled feet.

Jesus, who knew what it was like to sit on the throne, humbled Himself to kneel down on the floor and do this. And years later, His brother, who once hated, disbelieved, and tried to kill Him, picked up a pen to write the book of James. And when he put that pen to parchment and started writing out the very first words of this book, he wrote "*James, a **servant** of God and of the Lord Jesus Christ...*"

May I tell you what you have never met? You have never met a Christ-like person who was not a servant. I do not care if they carry a title like "reverend" or "pastor" or "bishop" or "elder" or "deacon" or "trustee." You have never met a Christ-like person who was not a servant.

James was a servant, and he put that in writing for us in the very first three words of this book. It is clear that there had been a radical change in the author of this book! But there had also been:

11

Changes in the audience

James 1:1 *James, a servant of God and of the Lord Jesus Christ, to the twelve tribes which are scattered abroad, greeting.*

If you have ever read many history books, you have probably come across the term "The Jews of the Diaspora." That word Diaspora is the word that James used here, it translates to our English word "scattered." We sometimes simply call it "the dispersion."

By the time that James wrote this book, not only had he been radically changed, his audience had also gone through truly radical changes. This book was not just written to Jews in general that had been scattered since the time of the Babylonian captivity. That is the position that Adam Clarke mistakenly takes:

> "To the Jews, whether converted to Christianity or not, who lived out of Judea, and sojourned among the Gentiles for the purpose of trade or commerce. At this time there were Jews partly traveling, partly sojourning, and partly resident in most parts of the civilized world; particularly in Asia, Greece, Egypt, and Italy. I see no reason for restricting it to Jewish believers only; it was sent to all whom it might concern," (6:798)

The reason he is clearly wrong is that James specifies over and over in multiple ways that he is talking to Jews that have been converted to Christianity. This entire book gives instructions that only a born-again child of God can truly fully follow. This book was written to Jews that had accepted Christ and then been scattered due to persecution. The Bible talks about that dispersion:

Acts 11:19 *Now they which were scattered abroad upon the persecution that arose about Stephen travelled as far as Phenice, and Cyprus, and Antioch, preaching the word to none but unto the Jews only.*

The Jews who had gotten saved on or shortly after Pentecost were settling down right there in Jerusalem. They were already in "mega-church mode." But Jesus had commanded them to take the gospel to every corner of the earth. You cannot exactly take the gospel to every corner of the earth, though, if all of you are hunkered down in one little corner of your own town!

So, God gave them a helpful "nudge" when He allowed a human tornado named Saul of Tarsus to come right through the middle of their trailer park, and they ended up scattering like debris in the wind. These are the people that James was writing to.

These people had lost most everything. They had been forced to run for their lives, leave possessions behind, and find shelter wherever they could. We have no reason to doubt that they were honest and faithful Christians while they were there in Jerusalem. But what they were not was passionate worldwide soul winners. God had to radically change the audience of James using the tool of persecution.

As you read and study the book of James, remember that you are dealing with people that had had their worlds turned upside down. That is one thing that makes this book so very remarkable. Normally when people have been through trials and tragedies, everyone coddles and comforts them. Please do not misunderstand me; there is most certainly a time and a place to comfort those who are hurting. But in general, James was not a coddling and comforting kind of person. James was more of a "Suck it up, Buttercup" kind of person. And there is something essential we can learn from what James wrote to these scattered, hurting people.

The thing we can learn from this is that hard times are no excuse to lower our expectations of ourselves.

Let me put that on paper one more time: hard times are no excuse to lower our expectations of ourselves.

If we have somehow gotten to where we expect less of ourselves than what God expects of us, our expectations of ourselves are too low.

I know people hurt. I know what it is like to be hurt. But we just happen to be in the middle of the war of the ages, the battle between good and evil, and we do not really have time to whimper and moan and give ourselves a pass on the things that

13

God expects of us. The hardest book in the Bible was written to people who had gone through hardships! Yet God did not lower His expectations of them so much as an inch.

The year was 1996, the place was the summer Olympic games being held in Atlanta, Georgia. The U.S. Ladies' Olympic gymnastics team had had great individual athletes before, some of them had even won individual gold medals. But never before in history had they ever won a team gold medal.

But this year it looked like nothing could stop them. They were in first place with a commanding lead over the second place Russians, and they were on the final event, the vault.

But then the pressure got to them, and they started to make mistakes. The first four of them to vault had really sloppy landings. And then things got even worse. One of their very best, Dominique Moceanu, fell twice in a row.

But if they thought things could not possibly get worse, they were sadly mistaken. Their very last vaulter, Kerri Strug, fell on her first vault. But to make things horribly, infinitely worse, when she fell, she tore two ligaments in her ankle.

The gold medal was gone. There was no hope.

Except for the fact that, when she hobbled over to her coach, the famous Bela Karolyi, he looked her in the eye and said, "Kerri, we need you to go one more time. We need you one more time for the gold."

She was crying. She was in agony. She had two torn ligaments.

That hurting, sobbing girl, limped her way back to the starting line. When the signal was given, she took off running. Last vault, last chance. She launched herself off of the springboard and high into the air, twisting, flipping, turning... and stuck a perfect landing on both feet, then immediately pulled her injured leg up into the air, and stood there balancing on one foot.

Then she collapsed and had to be carried off of the mat. A few moments later the judges came back with her score: 9.712, enough for the Americans to win their first ever team gold medal.

All that over a medal in a sporting event. So, let me say it again about things in the much more important arena of the spiritual life: *hard times are no excuse to lower our expectations of ourselves.*

James knew that, and he wanted his readers to know it.

James had been radically changed. His audience had been radically changed. He wrote a book to them demanding even more radical change.

Pay attention; God expects us to change from what we are into what He wants. James did. And the thing that changed him was getting floored by the realization that Jesus had risen from the dead and was exactly who He said He was. We serve a risen Savior; let's live like it.

Chapter Two
Setting the Standard for Suffering Saints

James 1:2 *My brethren, count it all joy when ye fall into divers temptations; 3 Knowing this, that the trying of your faith worketh patience. 4 But let patience have her perfect work, that ye may be perfect and entire, wanting nothing. 5 If any of you lack wisdom, let him ask of God, that giveth to all men liberally, and upbraideth not; and it shall be given him. 6 But let him ask in faith, nothing wavering. For he that wavereth is like a wave of the sea driven with the wind and tossed. 7 For let not that man think that he shall receive any thing of the Lord. 8 A double minded man is unstable in all his ways. 9 Let the brother of low degree rejoice in that he is exalted: 10 But the rich, in that he is made low: because as the flower of the grass he shall pass away. 11 For the sun is no sooner risen with a burning heat, but it withereth the grass, and the flower thereof falleth, and the grace of the fashion of it perisheth: so also shall the rich man fade away in his ways. 12 Blessed is the man that endureth temptation: for when he is tried, he shall receive the crown of life, which the Lord hath promised to them that love him.*

I said in the last chapter that James was a "Suck it up, Buttercup" kind of guy. That will manifest itself in these verses. Be aware, it is not that James was cold-hearted and had no compassion. As you read the book of James, it is clear that he saw a great deal of weakness and wrongdoing among the saints. And this was only a short time after Christianity had begun! There were almost certainly still Christians alive who had actually seen the risen Christ, and yet, the decay had already

17

begun. James knew that if someone did not whip things into shape, the church would eventually weaken to the point of being completely ineffective for Christ. So, James ended up being one of the people that gave the medicine people needed to go along with the spoonful of sugar that they wanted. So, let us consider that in this next section of verses.

A startling word

James 1:2 *My brethren, count it all joy when ye fall into divers temptations;*

There are two words we need to define right here and now in order to begin looking at what this verse means. The first one is the word "divers." It has nothing to do with swimming pools or backflips. It means "various kinds." We get our modern word "diverse" from it.

The second word we need to define is the word "temptations." Let me teach you something. This is one word that has two very different definitions to it. A modern example of that would be our word "gay." In 2018, gay can still mean "happy," as it always has, but it can also now mean "Steve is looking really inappropriately at Bubba, and I think he is about to try and hold his hand." One word, two definitions. How in the world do we know which one is which? Context, always context.

I am about to make you, my readers, hate me by putting something into your heads that you will still be struggling to get out of your heads days from now. Does anyone remember the theme song to *The Flintstones*?

"Flintstones, meet the Flintstones; they're a modern stone age family. From the town of Bedrock, they're a page right out of history. Let's ride with the family down the street, through the courtesy of Fred's own feet. Flintstones, meet the Flintstones, have a yabba-dabba-doo time, a dabba-doo-time, we'll have a gaaaaaaaayyyyyy ooooooollllllddddd tiiiiiiimmmmmeeeeee."

Have you ever so much as even blinked over that last line? No. The entire context of the song will tell you that there is nothing going on between Fred and Barney, everyone is just happy. But on the other hand, if you hear someone say, "Steve is marching in the gay pride parade," then the context of that statement will let you know that Steve has a fairly serious sin problem.

The word temptation in the Bible can either mean "testing and trials, hard times," or it can mean "being enticed to sin." It is only one word, but that one word has two very different meanings. That is very essential for us to understand in the book of James, right from this very first chapter, because the word temptation is going to be used both of those two ways in very near proximity to each other, and if you do not understand that there is a difference, and which is which, you will be extremely confused.

In verse two we find James talking about temptation. He said:

James 1:2 *My brethren, count it all joy when ye fall into divers temptations;*

Just from the context of this one verse, what kind of temptation is James talking about? He is either saying, "Be joyful about the fact that you are going through hard times," or he is saying, "Be joyful about the fact that you feel like getting drunk and looking at pornography while beating your children." Which one do you think it is?

James is certainly not telling us to be joyful about the fact that our flesh is tempted to sin. But what he is telling us is almost as startling. James was writing to people, some of whom had lost everything and were being hunted for their lives, saying *count it all joy... be joyful that you are going through trials.*

Does that sound as startling to you as it does to me? You see, it does not have an expiration date. What he said to Christians then applies to Christians now. I cannot think of a single time in which it is *natural* for us to feel this way. What James is asking is not natural; it is going to have to be something we choose to do when we naturally do not want to. The good news is, James quickly proceeded to give us some motivation to get us to do so.

James 1:3 *Knowing this, that the trying of your faith worketh patience.*

19

That word trying means "to put to the test" like a jeweler will put metal to the test by fire to see if it is real gold or silver. Real precious metals react very differently to fire than worthless metals do. In fact, real precious metals are actually improved by fire. Gold and silver are malleable. When I, as a goldsmith, wanted to bend gold or silver into a particular shape, the very first thing I would do was put the torch to it, bring it to a glowing red, and then let it cool slowly. After that, I could bend it to my will. That is the picture that James is beginning to draw. When we go through trials, the hardest of hard times, there is actually a benefit to them. Trials work in us to produce patience. They make us bendable and moldable in God's hands. This is something that James knew we would desperately need, so he emphasized it again and again:

James 1:4 *But let patience have her perfect work, that ye may be perfect and entire, wanting nothing.*

James 5:7 *Be patient therefore, brethren, unto the coming of the Lord. Behold, the husbandman waiteth for the precious fruit of the earth, and hath long patience for it, until he receive the early and latter rain.*

James 5:8 *Be ye also patient; stablish your hearts: for the coming of the Lord draweth nigh.*

James 5:10 *Take, my brethren, the prophets, who have spoken in the name of the Lord, for an example of suffering affliction, and of patience.*

James 5:11 *Behold, we count them happy which endure. Ye have heard of the patience of Job, and have seen the end of the Lord; that the Lord is very pitiful, and of tender mercy.*

Clearly, it is important that we earn patience. You say, "Sir, you misspoke. You meant to say 'learn patience.'" No, actually, I did not. It would be very nice if patience was actually something we could *learn* from a book. But it usually is not. Patience is something we *earn* by going through trials in the right manner. What do I mean by that? Look at the next verse:

James 1:4 *But let patience have her perfect work, that ye may be perfect and entire, wanting nothing.*

Let, meaning allow, patience to have her perfect work. What does that mean? Patience is being pictured as a schoolmaster, who is taking you through the school of trials. You can either bail out and quit, or you can continue on to the end of the course whether you like it or not. If you bail out and quit, you **learn** to quit, nothing more. But if you continue to do right during the trial, you **earn** infinitely more. You become patient by not quitting, by keeping on going through the fire. That type of school will make you complete (perfect and entire, wanting nothing) as a servant of God.

The people of the first century that James was writing to literally had this choice. Their trials were because they were following Christ. If they had just given up on that, they could have gone back to their normal lives, and everyone would have patted them on the back.

People now often have the exact same choice. There is usually a cost associated with following Christ.

When Hollywood stars "come out as Christians," the movie roles almost instantly stop coming in.

The fire chief down in Atlanta a few years ago was a great black gentleman named Kevin Cochran. He had been a firefighter since 1981, had risen to the rank of chief, and had always gotten excellent reviews. But then someone discovered that he had written a devotional booklet for the men at his church, taking a Biblical view of sexuality. He was then promptly fired for his faith.

But we still have it easy compared to most of the rest of the world. I sat in a meeting with a gentleman who had connections in the intelligence field. He told the story of how in Iraq, ISIS came to a Christian village and gave everyone a choice. Renounce Christ and convert to Islam or be slaughtered.

Two hours later, the first house they came to was asked their decision. They said they would not renounce Christ. The boy in the family was crucified, and the mother had her arms cut off, so she had to watch him die without being able to help him.

There will be unfathomable trials and heartaches that we have just for being a real Christian. Keep going, keep doing right, in fact, James told us to rejoice when we are hurting for being a Christian because God is molding us into something precious like a goldsmith molds metal.

21

A search for wisdom

James 1:5 *If any of you lack wisdom, let him ask of God, that giveth to all men liberally, and upbraideth not; and it shall be given him.*

This verse is certainly true in a general sense, but there is also a specific context surrounding it. In a general sense, wisdom is important and Biblical, and you should be praying for it in everything. But in the context of this passage, remember that we are dealing with people undergoing extremely hard trials. So, when James told them to ask God for wisdom, he seems to have had in mind wisdom concerning what they were going through.

During the good times, we may not have many questions. But I promise you, during the bad times, we are going to have a lot of questions. Why? What did I do? What should I do now? Who? How? When will it end? What purpose is there for this? I could go on and on, the potential questions are endless. We may not always get *answers* from our trials, but we can always get *wisdom* from our trials. God can make us smarter, better, more able to apply the knowledge that we do have, through the trials we undergo.

I have been power lifting for many years, and I love it. But a few years ago, I woke up with my right elbow in excruciating agony. Somehow the day before, I had done something bad to it while lifting. It was so bad I had to brush my teeth with my left hand, and when I sang, I held my microphone with my left hand. I had to wear a brace to the gym for weeks. But, finally, it got better.

I never did get an answer as to exactly how I did it. But what I did get was some wisdom. I went and studied proper lifting techniques, and I found four or five things I was doing wrong. I do not know which one of them caused my problem, but it does not matter, because I went ahead and changed all of them. My trial gave me wisdom.

That is a little thing, but the same principle holds true in big things. When we go through trials, we ought to use them as a time to learn what we have been doing wrong or maybe just what we could be doing better. We may never get all of the answers, but we will always get wisdom. God promised in this verse that He would give it, generously, and that He would not "upbraid" or chew us out! Have you ever asked someone for counsel and had them act like you were a bother to them? God never does that. You will always find Him excited about the prospect of making us wiser.

James 1:6 *But let him ask in faith, nothing wavering. For he that wavereth is like a wave of the sea driven with the wind and tossed.* **7** *For let not that man think that he shall receive any thing of the Lord.* **8** *A double minded man is unstable in all his ways.*

This all goes back to the asking for wisdom in verse five and then expecting God to give it to us. If we are going to ask for it, James reminds us that we need to ask without wavering. Wavering means "judging otherwise." In other words, if our lips are going to be asking God for wisdom, our hearts do not need to be saying, "But I know You won't do it!" We do not need to be going back and forth between belief and unbelief in the clear promises of God. A person that does that is like a wave of the sea, bouncing back and forth, coming and going, erratic and unstable. A person like that, doubting God yet trying to put God to the test anyway, is not going to get satisfactory results.

This is like an atheist standing in the town square and shouting, "Ok, God, if you strike me with lightning, I'll believe in You!" Is God going to answer that prayer? Not likely. God responds to faith not to goading. A person who prays but does not believe is not *trusting* God, he is *taunting* God. When you pray, believe what you are praying and to Whom you are praying!

A satisfaction wanted

James 1:9 *Let the brother of low degree rejoice in that he is exalted:*

When you see that word "brother," you know that James is speaking of the saved. James told the "brother of low degree," the brother with a low station in life, to rejoice in that he is exalted. You see, when a person gets saved, they become kings and priests (Revelation 1:5-6), joint heirs with Christ (Romans

8:17), and sons of God (John 1:12). That is quite a step up for people who are poor, uneducated, live in little shacks, and have menial jobs. People like that who get saved need to know they have a lot to be thankful for. In other words, they need to be satisfied with what they have been given in Christ, even if it never puts a scrap of gold in their pocket.

But James was not done with that egg yet. Now he would flip it over and cook the other side a while:

James 1:10 *But the rich, in that he is made low: because as the flower of the grass he shall pass away.* **11** *For the sun is no sooner risen with a burning heat, but it withereth the grass, and the flower thereof falleth, and the grace of the fashion of it perisheth: so also shall the rich man fade away in his ways.*

Just as the poor believer was to rejoice in that he was lifted up, the rich believer was to rejoice in that he was lowered down. But wait, doesn't the same thing happen to anyone who gets saved, rich or poor? Yes and no.

Everyone who gets saved gets forgiven of their sins, put into the family of God, and gets a reservation in Heaven. Everyone who gets saved gets the indwelling Holy Spirit. There is a great deal that is absolutely equal in salvation, no matter who you are or what your station in life is. But one thing that is different is that a well-off person who gets saved needs to be taught that their "well-offness" does not make them anything special to God. They need to be taught that all of that money is going to burn up. They need to be taught humility, and then they need to rejoice that they have been taught humility. Poor people do not usually have much of a high horse to come off of when they get saved, but rich people tend to have an entire *stable* of high horses which they ride to church every Sunday.

This is something that James will drill into the hearts of his readers throughout this book: your money does not make you an "extra special Christian" to God or the church. If it is done right, Christianity is the most equal thing in the world.

What is the summary of what James is saying in these verses? If God saved you as a poor person, and never lets you stop being poor, be satisfied. If God saved you as a rich person, and never treats you like a celebrity because you are rich but

24

treats you just like all of the poor people, be satisfied. As you might imagine, that is not exactly a popular message in today's prosperity gospel/Best Life Now/miracle water/private jet for Jesus mentality!

Even during times of trials, some Christians will do pretty well, and others will struggle. Either way God has been good, so be satisfied.

A standing welcomed

James 1:12 *Blessed is the man that endureth temptation: for when he is tried, he shall receive the crown of life, which the Lord hath promised to them that love him.*

James is still dealing with the subject of trials. And he will end this section with encouragement for those who determine to keep standing and keep doing right. There is a specific reward that we will be welcomed with for continuing to stand. There are several different crowns mentioned in the Bible that we can earn during our lifetimes of service for the Lord. For those who keep standing right even when times get tough, there is something called the Crown of Life. We do not know what it looks like or what precious stones are in it, but we do know that if it is a reward from God, it must be spectacular.

This will be one more thing for us to cast at His feet in heaven.

This crown is given to those that keep enduring, which according to the end of the verse is what people do who love Him. If you want to know who really loves the Lord and not just the goodies He gives, this is a pretty good indicator.

There was a time when Corrie Ten Boom had it very good as the daughter of a well-respected watchmaker in Holland and as the first female watchmaker in Holland. During those days, she did right. But there was a time when she did not have it so good, as a prisoner in a German concentration camp, having lost her father, her sister, everything.

During those times, she did right. She earned the Crown of Life, she loved the Lord enough not to let trials knock her out.

25

Just a few verses in, and I would say that James has done a pretty good job already of setting the standard for suffering saints.

There is not a normal human living that enjoys trials and tribulations. But there is also not a human living that will not go through trials and tribulations. They are universal, only the details change. That being the case, the only difference between people will be in how they choose to respond during times of trial and testing.

True story. Chippie, the parakeet, never saw it coming. One second, he was peacefully perched in his cage. The next he was sucked in, washed up, and blown over.

The problems began when Chippie's owner decided to clean Chippie's cage with a vacuum cleaner. She removed the attachment from the end of the hose and stuck it in the cage. The phone rang, and she turned to pick it up. She had barely said "hello" when "ssssopp!" Chippie got sucked in.

The bird owner gasped, put down the phone, turned off the vacuum, and opened the bag. There was Chippie–still alive but stunned.

Since the bird was covered with dust and soot, she grabbed him, raced to the bathroom, turned on the faucet, and held Chippie under the running water. Then, realizing that Chippie was soaked and shivering, she did what any compassionate bird owner would do . . . she reached for the hair dryer and blasted the pet with hot air.

Poor Chippie never knew what hit him.

A few days after the trauma, the reporter who had initially written about the event contacted Chippie's owner to see how the bird was recovering. "Well," she replied, "Chippie doesn't sing much anymore–he just sits and stares." (Lucado, 11)

I know things get hard during those trials. But singing is a whole lot better than sitting and staring, and way better than giving up on our Christian walk.

Chapter Three
The Telling Truth about Temptation

James 1:13 *Let no man say when he is tempted, I am tempted of God: for God cannot be tempted with evil, neither tempteth he any man: 14 But every man is tempted, when he is drawn away of his own lust, and enticed. 15 Then when lust hath conceived, it bringeth forth sin: and sin, when it is finished, bringeth forth death. 16 Do not err, my beloved brethren.*

I want to remind you of something that I said in the last chapter:

> The word temptation in the Bible can either mean "testing and trials, hard times," or it can mean "being enticed to sin." It is only one word, but that one word has two very different meanings. That is really essential for us to understand in the book of James, right from this very first chapter, because the word temptation is going to be used both of those two ways in very near proximity to each other, and if you don't understand that there is a difference, and which is which, you will be really really confused. (pg. 19)

In the last chapter we looked at verses two through twelve, and we saw James using the word temptations in regard to the testing and trials that God's people were going through. But now, right on the heels of that, he is going to use it the other way. When we read verses thirteen through sixteen, James had stopped talking about trials and hard times, and he had started talking about being enticed to sin. It seems as though thinking of the one made him think of the other since the same word is used for both. So, in these verses, James is going to deal with temptation in regard to our fleshly desire to do wrong and the devil's desire to entice us to do wrong.

A restriction

James 1:13 *Let no man say when he is tempted, I am tempted of God...*

Our society is very good at certain types of games. We Americans are very good at football and basketball and baseball and hockey and reasonably good at tennis and golf and bowling. But the game that our American society is the very best at is the blame game. Now, the blame game itself has been around for a very long time, in fact, it was the second game ever played in the history of humanity.

Does anyone know the first? That would be hide and seek.

But hard on the heels of hide and seek came the blame game:

Genesis 3:9 *And the LORD God called unto Adam, and said unto him, Where art thou?* **10** *And he said, I heard thy voice in the garden, and I was afraid, because I was naked; and I hid myself.* **11** *And he said, Who told thee that thou wast naked? Hast thou eaten of the tree, whereof I commanded thee that thou shouldest not eat?* **12** *And the man said, The woman whom thou gavest to be with me, she gave me of the tree, and I did eat.* **13** *And the LORD God said unto the woman, What is this that thou hast done? And the woman said, The serpent beguiled me, and I did eat.*

God gave a very simple command: do not eat the fruit of that tree. Eve ate the fruit. Adam ate the fruit. There is no need to decorate or garnish any of this; it really is that simple.

God came by and asked on whom the responsibility for the sin lay. Adam then immediately blamed Eve (It was that woman you gave me!).

God turned to Eve and asked her about all of this. Eve then immediately blamed the serpent (It was that dirty rotten snake, God!). That game has been played ever since, but nobody, **nobody** plays it as well as Americans:

If a woman spills hot coffee on herself at McDonald's, whose fault is it? It is McDonald's fault, of course, and they need to pay her millions of dollars.

If a man murders innocent children, whose fault is it? It is the gun manufacturers fault, of course.

If a teenager kills another kid, it is his parent's fault for not potty training him properly.

When Jesse Jackson Jr. embezzled millions of dollars, it was his bipolar disorder that made him do it.

When an ex-cop lunatic in California went on a killing spree, it was because "some kid thirty years ago in the first grade used a racial slur on him."

Yes, we Americans are the repeat, repeat, repeat champions of the world in the blame game, nobody else is even close, we are the Dream Team of the blame game. And that mentality has not stopped at the threshold of the church; it has kicked the doors open, barged in, and made itself right at home amongst the pews and hymnals.

And that makes what James said so essential for us to grasp. Look again at the restriction that he laid:

James 1:13 *Let no man say when he is tempted, I am tempted of God...*

Now, surely no one would actually do that, would they? Surely no one would blame their sin on God tempting them! I submit that they will only do so on days that end in "y."

A man commits adultery, and he blames God because "if God had made my wife prettier, and if He had made her more affectionate, I wouldn't have cheated!"

I read a news story on January 25, 2018, about a preacher in Wisconsin. He is being held for murder in the death of his wife, a murder that he attempted to make look like a suicide. The genius tried to hire a hitman on the dark web using bitcoins. They took his $6,000 and did absolutely nothing. Then he went out and bought a gun, drugged his wife, shot her in the head, and called the police and said that he found her that way.

When they got there, the gunshot wound was to the left side of her head. She is right-handed. She had no gunshot residue on her hands. He did. Even worse, all of the information about him trying to hire the hit-man was still on his computer. This man clearly has never watched so much as a single episode of CSI. The story went on to indicate that, basically, he was unhappy with her and wanted out and had had two affairs arranged on a website that I will not name.

That preacher bought into that. I looked at his picture and the picture of his wife, and it is very clear that he saw himself and his wife just like that commercial portrays. He had the "God, you didn't make my wife pretty enough, so this is your fault" attitude. (foxnews.com/us/2018/01/25)

Some teenager commits fornication, but it is God's fault because God made him desire beautiful girls, and He made those girls too beautiful to resist!

Someone shoplifts, and it is God's fault because if God had given what he or she wanted, they would not have had to shoplift to begin with.

Do you see how common this is? We could list thousands of examples. But James knew this was coming, and so he put an absolute restriction against it: when you are tempted to do wrong, do not blame God, ever, because He did not do it.

A girl we knew years ago was as loose and immoral as they come. Naturally, she ended up getting pregnant. Her mother's response was, "Well, clearly this is what God had in mind. Otherwise, she wouldn't have been granted this beautiful baby!" No, she slept around so consistently that she was bound to get pregnant and have a baby at some point. Stop blaming God for your daughter's loose ways!

God does NOT tempt people to sin.

A revelation

James 1:13b ...*for God cannot be tempted with evil, neither tempteth he any man:*

James has just made two statements comprising one revelation, and the first of those two statements is a very interesting one. He said that God cannot be tempted with evil. What does your mind immediately go to when you hear that?

Matthew 4:1 *Then was Jesus led up of the Spirit into the wilderness to be tempted of the devil. 2 And when he had fasted forty days and forty nights, he was afterward an hungred. 3 And when the tempter came to him, he said, If thou be the Son of God, command that these stones be made bread. 4 But he answered and said, It is written, Man shall not live by bread alone, but by every word that proceedeth out of the mouth of God. 5 Then the devil taketh him up into the holy city, and setteth him on a pinnacle of the temple, 6 And saith unto him, If thou be the Son of God, cast thyself down: for it is written, He shall give his angels charge concerning thee: and in their hands they shall bear thee up, lest at any time thou dash thy foot against a stone. 7 Jesus said unto him, It is written again, Thou shalt not tempt the Lord thy God. 8 Again, the devil taketh him up into an exceeding high mountain, and sheweth him all the kingdoms of the world, and the glory of them; 9 And saith unto him, All these things will I give thee, if thou wilt fall down and worship me. 10 Then saith Jesus unto him, Get thee hence, Satan: for it is written, Thou shalt worship the Lord thy God, and him only shalt thou serve.*

This is called the Wilderness Temptation of Christ. And the Bible says plainly that the devil came and tempted Him. And lest anyone think that this is an example of the innocent kind of temptation, meaning that Jesus was just going through trials and hard times, please pay attention to the fact that the devil was trying to get Jesus to fall down and worship him. Can we all agree that it is, in fact, evil to worship the devil?

And now please let me ask you to remember something else. Who is Jesus? The Son of God and God the Son. It is perfectly accurate to call Jesus God because He is, in fact, the second member of the Trinity. God the Father is God, God the Son is God, and God the Holy Spirit is God. So, when Jesus was being tempted to do evil, was God being tempted or not? Yes and no.

There are two sides to temptation. There is the enticer's side and the receiver's side. It is like this in every temptation. As we will see in a few moments, sometimes the enticer and the receiver are one and the same, but there is always an enticer's side and a receiver's side.

What do we mean by that? Let us illustrate by considering a rather unique food, mushrooms. Let's just say that I have with me a bowl of sautéed mushrooms. I come to wherever you are as you sit and read this book, and I wave that bowl of sautéed mushrooms under your nose. How many of my readers have I tempted? Some, yes, but certainly not all. There are many Philistines out there who have never learned to appreciate this most noble and delectable fungus.

But as far as I am concerned, I have tempted all of you! This is what we see in the temptation of Christ. Did the devil tempt Him? Yes. Was He tempted? No. You who are not interested in mushrooms, even though I tempted you, you could not be tempted. Jesus was not interested in sin, so even though the devil tempted Him, He could not be tempted. The enticer's side was there, but the receiver's side was not there. God cannot ever be interested in evil.

The second thing James said ties in with that and completes the revelation. Since God cannot be tempted with evil, since He is not interested in it, then He also cannot tempt man to do evil. It is an absolute impossibility for God to be the source of any temptation to evil that we face. Evil never interests Him either from the receiver's side or the enticer's side. He will never be on either the receiver's side of temptation or on the enticer's side of temptation. He is just not interested.

By the way, that ought to send up a helpful warning signal in your heart. Do you want God to be interested in you and interested in your needs and your desires? If you do, keep sin out of your life, because God is not interested in sin. It seems that we are producing a so-called Christianity in America where people expect to be allowed to wallow in sin of any kind and all kinds and yet still expect to have God standing nearby like an errand boy, just waiting for us to call and ask for something so He can hop right on that.

If that is your view of God, I personally very seriously doubt that you even know Him. God is not in the least bit interested in sin. He hates it. He will not tempt you to it, nor can He be tempted with it.

A reality
James 1:14 *But every man is tempted, when he is drawn away of his own lust, and enticed.*

Since God is never the source of temptation, James knew that it was necessary to tell us who or what is the source of temptation. In every single case, our own lust is ultimately the source.

"But what about the devil?" some will surely ask. Back in the 1970s, comedian Flip Wilson invented a female character named Geraldine Jones, and her famous line, her excuse for everything she did wrong was, "The devil made me do it." A great many people certainly take that view, so, is there anything to it?

We know quite well from Scripture that the devil is *often* the author of temptation. But he is not *always* the author of temptation. What is always true is that, whether the devil started things or whether he was absolutely oblivious to whatever is tempting us, our lust is *always* present.

When we see the word lust, we automatically think of sexual temptation. But that is only one application of a much broader word. The word lust is from the word *epithumia,* and it simply means *a strong craving or desire.* Notice that that definition does not even include anything about the word sin or wrong. There is a reason for that. Lust may or may not actually be wrong! In case that is a surprising concept to you, please look at this:

Galatians 5:17 *For the flesh lusteth against the Spirit, and the Spirit against the flesh: and these are contrary the one to the other: so that ye cannot do the things that ye would.*

The flesh lusts, it has extreme desires, but so does the Spirit. And the lust of the Spirit is contrary, opposite to the lust of the flesh. In other words, the flesh lusts for bad things, but the Spirit lusts for good things. The determining factor in whether lust is good or bad is whether or not you are lusting for something that is good or bad, something within limits or something off limits. Those extreme desires will always be with us; they are in us; they are a part of us. So, when the devil or a co-worker or a neighbor or a tv show or a stranger tempts us to do wrong, the devil may or may not be involved, but our own wrong desires are involved. God is not interested in sin, but we certainly are!

So here is what we know about a never, a sometimes, and an always:

God is NEVER behind our being tempted to sin.

The devil is SOMETIMES behind our temptation to sin.

Our lust is ALWAYS behind our temptation to sin.

Every single time we sin, bar none, the ultimate responsibility is not outward, but inward. Simply put, we do wrong because we want to! We have no right to play the blame game. We have no right to blame society or mama or the president or Hollywood or God or the devil; we do wrong because we want to, period. If we had no desire to do wrong, the devil himself could never make us do wrong. The reality is, we are responsible for it when we sin.

A reproduction

James 1:15 *Then when lust hath conceived, it bringeth forth sin: and sin, when it is finished, bringeth forth death.*

James used a very vivid word picture in this verse. He used the word conceived, like a father and mother that have produced a child. We often say that when people get married, they are going to "reproduce." Lust does the same thing, it reproduces, it conceives and gives birth.

Let us examine the stages in this verse.

James begins by giving us the conception stage, saying "when lust hath conceived." When our sinful lust is joined to a sinful temptation, a sinful conception takes place. Without both sides, there would be no conception, there would be nothing happening. If there is temptation without lust, nothing happens. If there is lust without temptation, nothing happens. But when there is both, and when we choose to put those two things

36

together, something happens. Lust, the "mother" in this occasion, the strong desire in our heart, conceives. It finds itself with an illegitimate child.

James secondly gives us the birth stage, saying "it bringeth forth sin." When our lust is allowed to join to a temptation, a conception takes place, and the conception is followed by a birth, the birth of a sin: a sinful action or a sinful attitude.

James then gives us the death stage, saying *and sin, when it is finished, bringeth forth death.*

Now think: does it seem like something was left out?

The normal life cycle is conception, birth, life, death. But notice that when we are talking about sin, **there is no "life!"** Sin does not produce life, it produces death. It kills something, every single time. It may kill a reputation or a home or a conscience or a nest egg or a friendship, or it may actually kill a person, either the person doing it or some innocent person that gets in the way. Sin always produces death.

That is a horrible paradigm. And there is really only one logical stage at which to stop it, and that is at the conception. Once the conception has occurred, once the temptation has been joined to the lust, everything is a done deal. There will be a birth, and there will be a death. So the place to stop that from happening is at the very start. Romans 13:14 puts it this way:

Romans 13:14 *But put ye on the Lord Jesus Christ, and make not provision for the flesh, to fulfil the lusts thereof.*

Paul was saying that we do not need to even give ourselves the chance to have our lust and our temptations meet up! This is why drunks have no business near alcohol. This is why a person who is being tempted to commit adultery does not need to work with or talk to or be online with the person that is tempting them to commit adultery. God is not interested in sin, but we are. We need to be proactive in not allowing our lusts to meet up with our temptations. And when we are surprised, like Joseph was with Mrs. Potiphar, we need to run! Lust reproduces, and what it reproduces is a killer.

I can take you to shuttered church buildings that used to be thriving congregations. There was a sinful conception in the pulpit or in the pews, and the death of a church occurred.

I could drive you by several houses and show you where families used to live; a father, a mother, children. Those families do not live there anymore. They do not even live together anymore. Someone started looking at pornography, or put liquor to their lips, or started talking to an old flame from high school, and that conceived sin brought about the death of those families.

A reminder

James 1:16 *Do not err, my beloved brethren.*

Let me summarize these few words for you. "Do NOT make a mistake on this one, my dear brothers."

Do not make the mistake of blaming God for your temptations!

Do not make the mistake of forgetting that you have wicked, lustful desires inside of you!

Do not make the mistake of allowing your lust and your temptations to get together!

Historian Shelby Foote tells of a soldier who was wounded at the battle of Shiloh during the American Civil War and was ordered to go to the rear. The fighting was fierce, and within minutes he returned to his commanding officer. "Captain, give me a gun!" he shouted. "This fight ain't got any rear!" (Daily Walk, July 10, 1993)

That is exactly how we need to view our battle against temptation. Stay armed against it at all times, never lay down your spiritual weapons, this fight "ain't got any rear."

We all carry our biggest problems inside of us every single day. We have wicked, lustful desires inside of us, and if we ever forget that, if we ever let our guard down, we are in trouble.

That is just *The Telling Truth About Temptation.*

Chapter Four
The Other Side of the Hinge

James 1:17 *Every good gift and every perfect gift is from above, and cometh down from the Father of lights, with whom is no variableness, neither shadow of turning.* **18** *Of his own will begat he us with the word of truth, that we should be a kind of firstfruits of his creatures.* **19** *Wherefore, my beloved brethren, let every man be swift to hear, slow to speak, slow to wrath:* **20** *For the wrath of man worketh not the righteousness of God.*

In our old church building, we had a kitchen. The door to that kitchen was unique in that it swung both ways. It had a double action hinge. It allowed you to exit the kitchen by pushing your way through the door, and it allowed you to enter the kitchen by pushing your way through the door. Or you could do either of those things by pulling the door to you from either direction.

The last verse of the last section acts as that type of a hinge between verses thirteen through fifteen and verses seventeen through twenty. Look at that hinge verse:

James 1:16 *Do not err, my beloved brethren.*

If you remember, here is the way I explained that verse:

> Let me summarize these few words for you. "Do NOT make a mistake on this one, my dear brothers."
>
> Do not make the mistake of blaming God for your temptations!

41

Do not make the mistake of forgetting that you have wicked, lustful desires inside of you!

Do not make the mistake of allowing your lust and your temptations to get together!

We all carry our biggest problems inside of us every single day. We have wicked, lustful desires inside of us, and if we ever forget that, if we ever let our guard down, we are in trouble.

That side of things told us what God would not do. But there is another side to that hinge verse, and it tells us what God will do and how we should respond because of that. We will call this chapter *The Other Side Of The Hinge*.

Let's begin by looking at verse sixteen once more and using it this time to look forward, not backward.

James 1:16 *Do not err, my beloved brethren.*

This still means "Do not make a mistake on this one." Only now we will be looking at the verses after rather than the verses before in order to find out what we should not be making a mistake on.

A gift and a giver

James 1:17 *Every good gift and every perfect gift is from above, and cometh down from the Father of lights, with whom is no variableness, neither shadow of turning.*

In verse thirteen, James was instructing his readers not to say that God was tempting them to do evil. He was dealing with people that regarded God as being a giver of something bad: temptation. Now on the other side of the hinge James is going to acknowledge that God is a giver, but what He gives is always good!

There are two adjectives that James used to describe the types of gifts that God gives. He gives gifts that are good and gifts that are perfect. Whatever gift we have that fits either of these descriptions, God is the author and giver of it. Good is from the word *agathos,* and it means "that which is excellent, pleasant, and agreeable." The second adjective used is perfect. It is from the word *telos,* and it means "complete." The gifts that

God gives are the best kind of gifts; they do not defile us or dirty us or leave us lacking.

James said that these are the kind of gifts that come from above, from Heaven, from God, not evil things like temptation.

When James got around to describing God the giver, he called Him the Father of lights. What did he mean? The Bible answers that question very early on:

Genesis 1:3 *And God said, Let there be light: and there was light.*

God is the Father of lights because He brought light into being, He made it. But what does that have to do with Him being the giver of every good and perfect gift? As we will see in the next few words, it has to do with the fact that He is utterly unchangeable, which means that all of His gifts will always be good.

James went on to describe God, the Father of lights, as being the One "with whom is no variableness, neither shadow of turning." Variableness is like a windshield wiper, going back and forth between positions. God is not like that; He always is what He always is. In fact, He is so unvarying that there is not even a "shadow of turning" with Him.

When a person stands very, very still, he may appear to be absolutely unmoving. But there is a way that we could actually detect movement, even very tiny movement. If we were to take a very powerful light and place it behind him, he would cast a very long shadow. If we were to go to the end of that shadow and stare down at it, we would notice something. If that man makes even a tiny movement, the shadow will move by several inches or maybe even by several feet. The moving shadow will be the give-away that the person that appears still is, in fact, moving.

But that is not so of God. He is so unmoving in His character that if you were to shine the entire sun behind Him and look at the end of a one million-mile-long shadow, it would not be moving.

Taking it back to Him not giving bad things like temptation and giving every good thing, James is saying that there will never be an exception to this. God will never, ever,

ever be the giver of a temptation for us to do evil, and He will always, always, always be the giver of every good gift.

When you are walking down the beach right at sunset, and you get to see that big orange ball touch the horizon and spread its last glorious rays of the day, have you ever considered the "good gifts" you are enjoying? Like, the feet you are walking on, the sun that is giving warmth and light, the ears that are hearing the gentle waves and the crying of the seagulls, and the eyes that are taking it all in.

God did that. God gave all of those good and perfect gifts.

When you hold a child and look in wonder at its precious little face smiling up at you, who do you think created life, that life, and allowed you those arms to hold that baby?

God did that. God gave all of those good and perfect gifts.

When you consider salvation, the resurrection, heaven, the reunion with saved loved ones we have waiting for us, who do you think conceived and planned all of that for us?

God did that. God gave all of those good and perfect gifts.

Every bite of food you take, every breath you breathe, every time your heart squeezes and pumps blood through your body, you ought to have "thank you, thank you, thank you" ringing through your heart.

A genesis and a goal

James 1:18 *Of his own will begat he us with the word of truth, that we should be a kind of firstfruits of his creatures.*

In the beginning, God created the heaven and the earth. He then made light, planets and stars, animals, and then man. He begat us; He brought us forth. Likewise, He later begat us in a spiritual sense, and that is what James is speaking of here. He willed us into existence by His spoken word in the beginning, and He wills us into the new birth with His spoken word while He walked among us and with His written word now. If we exist now physically, it is because God made it happen. If we come into spiritual existence as a born-again child of God, it is because He makes it happen.

But for what? Was this some random act with no end or purpose? Or was it something that had a purpose, but our "secretive and mysterious God" will not tell us what it is? No. It had a purpose, it has a purpose, and God was good enough in this very verse to tell us what that purpose is! He saved us so that we should be "a kind of firstfruits of His creatures."

What did James mean by that? These are not terms we use in our modern day, so they bear some explaining. When James referenced the first fruits, he was using a reference that his Jewish audience was very familiar with:

Leviticus 23:9 *And the LORD spake unto Moses, saying,* **10** *Speak unto the children of Israel, and say unto them, When ye be come into the land which I give unto you, and shall reap the harvest thereof, then ye shall bring a sheaf of the firstfruits of your harvest unto the priest:* **11** *And he shall wave the sheaf before the LORD, to be accepted for you: on the morrow after the sabbath the priest shall wave it.* **12** *And ye shall offer that day when ye wave the sheaf an he lamb without blemish of the first year for a burnt offering unto the LORD.* **13** *And the meat offering thereof shall be two tenth deals of fine flour mingled with oil, an offering made by fire unto the LORD for a sweet savour: and the drink offering thereof shall be of wine, the fourth part of an hin.* **14** *And ye shall eat neither bread, nor parched corn, nor green ears, until the selfsame day that ye have brought an offering unto your God: it shall be a statute for ever throughout your generations in all your dwellings.*

When the Jews began to bring in the harvest, they would bring the very first part and offer it to the Lord. That first part was not the harvest, it was simply the tip of the iceberg, and it was a sign of much greater things to come. So, when James wrote to his audience of suffering Jewish believers in Christ, and when he told them that they were the first fruits, he was pointing them to the fact that God was going to bring in an enormous harvest of Gentile believers! James did not want them, the Jewish believers, to think that they were "it." He wanted them to be glad about the fact that they were the tip of the iceberg of the millions of people that were going to come to the saving knowledge of Jesus Christ, most of whom would be Gentiles.

This was the will of God, this was why He "begat" them. And the same thing still holds true for us today. When we get saved, God expects us to be just the tip of the iceberg. He expects us to go out and bring in a great harvest to God, not all of which will be like us. In fact, a great many of them may be very different from us. But just like the Jews were to rejoice in the salvation of the Gentiles, we Gentiles are supposed to be rejoicing in the salvation of others who are different from ourselves. *It is the goal of God to win the world to Himself and to use us to do it.*

When we were kids, we would often go swimming at a place called Maple Springs. Before they would let us get into the water, the adults sat us all down and gave us some instructions. Naturally, there was "don't pee in the pool" like any little kid would EVER do that...

But the last thing they always said to us was "Now pick a buddy, and make sure you stay together at all times."

In a spiritual sense, do you understand what God is commanding us? "Okay, you are saved now; you get to go to heaven. But I do not want anyone coming alone. Everybody go win a buddy and bring him or her with you."

Who was it that loved you enough to win you to the Lord? Do you remember? Have you ever thought of where you would be if they had not?

Go do the same! Win somebody to Christ and bring them to heaven with you.

A guard and a grief

James 1:19 *Wherefore, my beloved brethren, let every man be swift to hear, slow to speak, slow to wrath:*

When you see that word "wherefore" in the Bible, know that it means "because of this." It will be a reference to what came before it, what has already been said. It is going to call for a decision based on the arguments that have been presented. James had just finished telling his readers that God was never the author of temptation, He is always the author of good, and

46

that He saved them for a specific purpose. That purpose was so that they could turn and win the Gentile world to God. God wanted them to be soul winners and to bring in a massive harvest.

That was going to require something. Just like a farmer would have requirements before he could harvest (oxen, yokes, sickles), believers have some requirements before we can reap our harvest as well. In this case, James was going to lay a requirement on them in the form of a guard. He told them to guard themselves in three areas: their listening, their speaking, and their temperament.

Without even much explanation or exposition, you have already most likely discerned that these three areas are huge and that if we can guard ourselves in them, we will very likely be incredibly effective for God. And you are correct.

The first thing James told us was to guard ourselves by being swift to hear. To hear who? Yes. Whoever you insert, yes. Obviously, we are to be swift to hear God. If there is anyone we are to be very, very swift to hear, we need to be swift to hear God. We need to be listening very carefully to His Word, the Bible. We need to be listening very carefully to Him speaking to our hearts in prayer. We need to be listening very carefully to the urgings of the Holy Spirit.

Our responsibility to be swift to hear does not stop with God, though, it also extends to man. We are to be swift to hear the people that God has placed in positions of spiritual authority: pastors, teachers, evangelists.

But our responsibility to be swift to hear does not stop with God, or even with good men. Listen to me very carefully; it also extends even to lost men. You see, if we are going to win the lost to Jesus, we cannot do so by rudeness. If we interrupt and brush people off and dominate a conversation, we will win our arguments and lose our chance to save souls. There are people who could best be described as "Jerks for Jesus." Do not be one of those.

No, we cannot entertain heresy, that is not what James is saying. But we must be willing to politely listen to those who are lost, in the wrong, and have given us the chance to talk to them about the right. We need to speak, we need to tell people all of the right things and the truth of the gospel. Listening alone will never win a soul, but not listening will never win a soul either!

The second thing James told us was to guard ourselves by being slow to speak. Notice that he did not tell us not to speak; he told us to be slow to speak. He was warning against impetuous outbursts. Words can do an incredible amount of damage, and if we just shoot off our mouths without considering our words, we will more likely send people to Hell than bring them to Heaven.

Preachers should beware of this. Because we speak all the time, we can become very careless with our words. We must not, ever. There is a preacher that is famed around this country and booked up for years in advance. But he will never be allowed to preach in our church while I am the pastor because he has no filter between his brain and his mouth. If it pops into his head, it pops out of his mouth automatically, and he has hurt tons and tons of people. I will go so far as to say that he is responsible for sending a great number of people to Hell. A sinner will come into a meeting where he is preaching, and if they do not look right, he is more likely to insult them than he is to win them.

But it is not just preachers because James was not writing to preachers. This applies to everyone. Every one of us should be slow to speak, we should do our best to choose our words carefully and speak only the words that Christ would have us speak. Does this mean that we will never be offensive or hurt any feelings? Quite the contrary. *Christ was often very offensive, and He hurt a ton of feelings*. But He did so simply by telling the truth not by saying things that were dirty or stupid.

The third thing James told us was to guard ourselves in the area of our temper. He told us to be slow to wrath. Now please note, he did not tell us never to get angry. Those that tell you to never get angry have not read their Bibles very carefully:

Ephesians 4:26 *Be ye angry, and sin not: let not the sun go down upon your wrath:* **27** *Neither give place to the devil.*

This was a command of God. We are to get angry! But we are not to sin. There are things in which, if we do not get angry, we have sinned by our non-anger. For instance, when a man's wife is being assaulted, he should get very angry, very quickly, and with a very large caliber.

Jesus Himself got angry:

John 2:13 *And the Jews' passover was at hand, and Jesus went up to Jerusalem,* **14** *And found in the temple those that sold oxen and sheep and doves, and the changers of money sitting:* **15** *And when he had made a scourge of small cords, he drove them all out of the temple, and the sheep, and the oxen; and poured out the changers' money, and overthrew the tables;* **16** *And said unto them that sold doves, Take these things hence; make not my Father's house an house of merchandise.* **17** *And his disciples remembered that it was written, The zeal of thine house hath eaten me up.*

Yes, Jesus got angry! In fact, He got "table flipping, scourge making, posterior-whipping angry!" But did He sin? Certainly not.

When James spoke of anger, he did not tell us to never get angry, he told us to be slow to anger. In other words, if every little thing sets you off, you are going to be the world's worst soul winner. You will never accomplish God's purpose for your life if you have a short fuse. *If you are quick to anger, the devil will make sure that there is always some little thing for you to blow up at right when a sinner is watching you.* We have to guard ourselves in these three areas!

James would follow up that thought with one final comment on our anger:

James 1:20 *For the wrath of man worketh not the righteousness of God.*

If our anger is God's anger, our anger will work the righteousness of God. In other words, if we only get angry at the things that God gets angry at, we will be just fine. But if we get angry at the things that we normally get angry at, insults, bad drivers, a kid breaks the vase with Granny's ashes in it, then we can be very certain of not being able to capably fulfill God's purpose for saving us.

Do not err, my beloved brethren. Do not forget where our good gifts come from and do not forget why we are here and what our purpose is.

Chapter Five
Mirror, Mirror

James 1:21 *Wherefore lay apart all filthiness and superfluity of naughtiness, and receive with meekness the engrafted word, which is able to save your souls.* **22** *But be ye doers of the word, and not hearers only, deceiving your own selves.* **23** *For if any be a hearer of the word, and not a doer, he is like unto a man beholding his natural face in a glass:* **24** *For he beholdeth himself, and goeth his way, and straightway forgetteth what manner of man he was.* **25** *But whoso looketh into the perfect law of liberty, and continueth therein, he being not a forgetful hearer, but a doer of the work, this man shall be blessed in his deed.* **26** *If any man among you seem to be religious, and bridleth not his tongue, but deceiveth his own heart, this man's religion is vain.* **27** *Pure religion and undefiled before God and the Father is this, To visit the fatherless and widows in their affliction, and to keep himself unspotted from the world.*

Mirrors are designed for a specific purpose, namely, to look into them, see what needs "fixing," and fix it. But so often they are used for every purpose but that.

I am reminded of a story I heard many years ago about a high school that was having a problem. It seems that the "cool" thing for the girls to do was to go into their restroom, put on the brightest red lipstick they owned and kiss the mirror. Naturally, there was at least one person in school who hated that trend: the school janitor. Lipstick is, well, sticky, and therefore very hard to clean off of a surface like that. These girls were making his life miserable. He appealed for them to stop, but it just kept happening. Finally, with the principal's permission, he figured out a solution to the problem. He and the principal got several of the more popular girls, who just so happened to be the ringleaders in all of this, to come into the restroom after the mirror had been smooched one day. Once they arrived, the principal said, "Girls, we have asked you to stop doing this, and yet it persists. Mr. Feeney here is the janitor, and you are making his life miserable."

The girls just smirked at that, and their faces sent a clear message of "So? Like we care."

The principal continued. "I want you to see just how difficult it is for him to clean this mirror each day after you have done this. Mr. Feeney, please show the girls what you have to go through."

The humble janitor nodded his head, took out his squeegee, dipped it in a toilet, and proceeded to clean the mirror.

Problem solved.

James lived in a time period when there were mirror problems as well, albeit of a different sort. Let's get into our text and see what was going on.

A removal of the residue

James 1:21 *Wherefore lay apart all filthiness and superfluity of naughtiness, and receive with meekness the engrafted word, which is able to save your souls.*

Let me jog your memory again as we begin this section. When James wrote this letter, to whom was he writing, the lost or the saved?

The saved. James was writing to people who were absolutely born again.

So that being the case, why did he have to tell them, the saved, Christians, to lay aside filthiness? Since we clearly know what that word filthiness means, the next phrase will help it to make sense. That next phrase is "superfluity of naughtiness."

I am betting none of you have used that phrase in your daily speech in the last few, forever. But doesn't it kind of sound like something that needs to be said in a British accent? *Superfluity of naughtiness...*

What is superfluity of naughtiness? That phrase means "The leftover, residual naughtiness from before you got saved."

You see, when we get saved, we get saved all the way. From the moment you accept Christ you are fully, utterly redeemed.

But getting *saved* all the way does not equal getting *sanctified* all the way. We still have flesh.

If I can go back about twenty years or so to the Disney Aladdin movie, it is kind of like when the genie described his lot in life as "infinite cosmic power... itty bitty living space."

That is us, the saved. We have the Holy Spirit of God indwelling us, empowering us, and yet the vessel that is our flesh is still weak and wicked. We are saved, but there is something else we need. Getting saved will get us to heaven, but we still need something more for the rest of the time we are here on earth. That something more is called sanctification; being set aside for His use. Being drawn out of that which is base and common and being elevated to that which is high and holy.

How in the world does that happen? Here is your answer: it is the Word of God, the Bible, taken into our system on a daily basis that must do that. But notice that it is not just the "heard" word that does it, but the "engrafted word."

How many of you are a little bit familiar with the grafting of plants and trees? That is the picture that James is drawing here. Let me tell you a bit about it. In the grafting process, the flesh of a tree branch will be wounded; it will be cut partially open. Then a branch from a different tree will be cut to fit, placed in the open wound, bound up, and allowed to grow into that tree.

That is the picture James is using, and it is absolutely perfect. When you read and study the Bible or when you listen to the preaching of the Bible, if you will do as the next phrase says, if you will receive it with meekness, do you know what it will do?

The first thing it will do is wound you. It will cut, and it will hurt. But the next thing it will do is grow into that wound and end up producing fruit in your life that never would have been possible any other way. When a born-again person cannot seem to get any victory over sin, I know that there is a very high likelihood that they are not really taking the time and absorbing vast quantities of Scripture. The engrafted word will sanctify you.

Notice the last phrase, and the argument James draws from it. He says, *"and receive with meekness the engrafted word, which is able to save your souls."* His argument is that, since the Word of God is powerful enough to save your soul, it is also powerful enough to sanctify you and remove the sinful residue left over from before you got saved.

A right reception

James 1:22 *But be ye doers of the word, and not hearers only, deceiving your own selves. 23 For if any be a hearer of the word, and not a doer, he is like unto a man beholding his natural face in a glass: 24 For he beholdeth himself, and goeth his way, and straightway forgetteth what manner of man he was. 25 But whoso looketh into the perfect law of liberty, and continueth therein, he being not a forgetful hearer, but a doer of the work, this man shall be blessed in his deed.*

Verse twenty-two is probably the most famous verse in the book of James:

James 1:22 *But be ye doers of the word, and not hearers only, deceiving your own selves.*

The Bible cannot deceive you, but you can deceive you. And one of the main ways you can do that is by hearing the Bible and stopping at that. If all you do is hear, but you do not apply, you have deceived yourself.

This is a funny thing that you often see in, of all places, the gym. There will be some scrawny twig that gets interested in being the next Incredible Hulk. He will read and watch videos and ask advice and learn so much of the subject that he can tell you about odd exercises and who invented them. He can tell you the name of every supplement on the market, he can tell you how much protein you need to take in each day based on your body weight, and he even walks around the gym with his arms popped out to the side like he has huge lats when he has none. Do you know what has happened? He knows a lot, but knowing is not the same as doing. Imaginary lat syndrome is not the same as actually having lats.

We can take the right first step, we can absorb vast quantities of Scripture, but if we do not move it from our head to our hands and feet, we have still accomplished nothing.

Look at verse twenty-three again:

James 1:23 *For if any be a hearer of the word, and not a doer, he is like unto a man beholding his natural face in a glass:* (a mirror)

Verse twenty-three is about a mirror. When we look in one, we see ourselves like we really are. That tool, the mirror, is designed to help us make changes.

But have you ever known people who, it was very clear were ignoring the message in the mirror? *Pardon me, sir, that entire "speedo thing" is not working for you as you waddle down the beach in all of your flabby, wrinkled, pasty white jiggly glory.*

A person who looks into God's Word on the surface then sees their problems and walks away unwilling to change, is like a person who does that.

They say, "I'm okay because I looked into the mirror!"

But verse twenty-five tells us what the mirror is really for and how it is supposed to change us:

James 1:25 *But whoso looketh into the perfect law of liberty, and continueth therein, he being not a forgetful hearer, but a doer of the work, this man shall be blessed in his deed.*

Notice the description given of Scripture. It is called "the perfect **law** of **liberty**." Have you ever paid attention to those two terms and considered them as they are somehow joined together in this one phrase? At first blush it seems like they would not go together at all, doesn't it? "Law" and "liberty."

But not only do they go together, one is actually wholly dependent upon the other. Our forefathers here in America actually knew this. Do you remember a phrase in one of our great patriotic songs? "Confirm thy soul in self-control, thy liberty in law."

Confirm thy liberty in law. It sounds like they were saying the same thing James was saying.

And they were. Without law, there is no liberty.

A few years ago, I got into an argument with an idiotic anarchist, and yes, I know I am being redundant. He and they believe that "the best government is no government." They actually think that law and liberty cannot co-exist.

But let me get you to think this through. Ladies, if there is no law against rape, then do you actually have liberty? You who have jobs, if there is no law against your employer making you work 60 hours a week and then not paying you, do you actually have liberty? You who have homes, if there is no law allowing you to have and protect your own private property, do you actually have liberty? You who drive, if people are allowed to drive full speed down the wrong side of the road and slam into your car with you and your kids in it, do you actually have liberty?

No, no, no, no. For there to actually be liberty, there has to be law. That is exactly what James is saying in the spiritual sense. Yes, the Word of God is "the law" to Christians. We are bound to obey what God has commanded us in the Bible. But the Bible, the law, is the "perfect law of liberty" to us! In other words, the more we submit ourselves to obey the Bible and make it the law of our lives, the freer we become! *"Whoso looketh into the perfect law of liberty, and continueth therein, he being not a forgetful hearer, but a doer of the work, this man shall be **blessed** in his deed."*

Whoever binds himself to obey the commands of God given to Christians in the Bible will find himself blessed of God, and there is no greater freedom than that!

I obey the Bible, and it has made me free. I am free from guilt; I am not doing anything that keeps me awake at night. I am free from having to write checks to lawyers to try and get me out of trouble. I am free from wondering if there is some other little Wagner that I do not know about running around out there. I am free from hangovers. I am free from drug addiction. As I obey the Bible, God is using it to sanctify me, and I am free.

A real righteousness

James 1:26 *If any man among you seem to be religious, and bridleth not his tongue, but deceiveth his own heart, this man's religion is vain.* **27** *Pure religion and undefiled before God and the Father is this, To visit the fatherless and widows in their affliction, and to keep himself unspotted from the world.*

Notice that word "seem." It is entirely possible for a person not to actually *be* religious, but to absolutely *seem* religious.

I preached a revival in a small town in West Virginia some years ago. The pastor I was with took me around the area on a little tour. We passed by an old, venerable-looking Catholic church. The priest was a very traditional, robe and vestment wearing priest. Everything about him and the church seemed very religious.

Except for the fact that a week or so before I got there, the local sheriff picked him up stoned drunk and passed out on a park bench.

But that is not just a Catholic thing. Up in Virginia, a Baptist pastor ended up getting exposed as a long-term drunk after crashing his car into a tree in someone's front yard. Turns out the deacons had been covering for him for years.

Like I said, it is entirely possible for a person not to actually *be* religious but to absolutely *seem* religious.

Thinking of that, James brought up the issue of that most troublesome body part, the tongue. The tongue is perhaps the best indicator of righteousness or unrighteousness. Here is why I say that:

Matthew 15:18 *But those things which proceed out of the mouth come forth from the heart; and they defile the man.*

Our mouth is a giveaway to our heart. And it is often true that people "deceive themselves" about their righteousness when their tongue consistently gives away their unrighteousness.

A man like that may have religion, but James says that that man's religion is "vain." It is empty of any real substance. It looks good on the outside, but there is no meat to it.

Notice in verse twenty-seven WHO the real judge of righteousness is:

James 1:27 *Pure religion and undefiled before God and the Father is this...*

We can protest all we like, but God and the Father is the judge of whether or not we really have what James calls "pure religion." He sets the standard on it. That is the who, but what about the "what?"

Now notice WHAT it is:

James 1:27 *Pure religion and undefiled before God and the Father is this, To visit the fatherless and widows in their affliction, and to keep himself unspotted from the world.*

Notice, please notice, that there are two components to pure religion and that this is not a "multiple choice test." It is not an either/or. Pure religion consists both of service and sanctification. As an example of service, James points to tending to the fatherless and widows. And he goes right from that into saying *"and to keep himself unspotted from the world."*

In other words, a person who visits nursing homes and orphanages and feeds the homeless, and also drinks and curses and sleeps with someone they are not married to does not have pure religion.

On the flip side, a person who never curses, never drinks, is 100% faithful to his spouse, and yet never serves those in need also does not have pure religion.

Pure religion consists both of sanctification and service. Religion is NOT salvation; but if you are saved, you should be looking into the mirror of God's Word and becoming more and more religious, more and more service oriented, more and more sanctified from sin to God.

Take a look in the mirror: what do you see?

Chapter Six
Rolling Out or Rolling Up the Red Carpet

James 2:1 *My brethren, have not the faith of our Lord Jesus Christ, the Lord of glory, with respect of persons.* **2** *For if there come unto your assembly a man with a gold ring, in goodly apparel, and there come in also a poor man in vile raiment;* **3** *And ye have respect to him that weareth the gay clothing, and say unto him, Sit thou here in a good place; and say to the poor, Stand thou there, or sit here under my footstool:* **4** *Are ye not then partial in yourselves, and are become judges of evil thoughts?* **5** *Hearken, my beloved brethren, Hath not God chosen the poor of this world rich in faith, and heirs of the kingdom which he hath promised to them that love him?* **6** *But ye have despised the poor. Do not rich men oppress you, and draw you before the judgment seats?* **7** *Do not they blaspheme that worthy name by the which ye are called?* **8** *If ye fulfil the royal law according to the scripture, Thou shalt love thy neighbour as thyself, ye do well:* **9** *But if ye have respect to persons, ye commit sin, and are convinced of the law as transgressors.*

We have made our way through the first chapter of James. We have found James writing to hurting and dispersed Christians. And while he is writing in love, he is also not pulling any punches. James is giving them the straight truth on how they, and we, ought to be behaving. He will continue that in chapter two and will begin by addressing a problem that I am guessing he found to be very surprising given the circumstances.

A foul mixture

James 2:1 *My brethren, have not the faith of our Lord Jesus Christ, the Lord of glory, with respect of persons.*

As James begins this section, he addresses the readers once more as brethren. So once again he is identifying his audience as saved people, specifically saved Jews. They have been convicted of their sins; they have been washed in the blood; they are born again; they are new creatures in Christ. In other words, when you read the last phrase of the verse, they are people who ought to know better. These born-again Christians had a very foul mixture going on; they were saved, but in this particular thing they were behaving the same way that lost people behave. They were having what James calls "respect of persons."

That phrase bears some explaining. We know that respecting people, as we use the term respect in our modern day, is a good thing. We teach children to respect their parents, and we should.

We teach church members to respect their pastor, and we should. How in the world do parents ever expect the pastor to be able to help their children through his preaching and pastoring when they have taught them to disrespect him?

We teach wives to respect their husbands, and we should. How in the world will kids ever respect dad when dad is not respected by mom?

We teach soldiers to respect their superiors, and we should.

That kind of respect is perfectly acceptable and Biblical. James had a different kind of thing in mind, though, and he is not the first one in the Bible that dealt with this kind of "respect:"

Acts 10:34 *Then Peter opened his mouth, and said, Of a truth I perceive that God is no respecter of persons:* **35** *But in every nation he that feareth him, and worketh righteousness, is accepted with him.*

You may not know what is going on in this passage when Peter spoke these words. It makes a huge difference, so you need to know.

Peter had just been taught, by God Himself, that God was going to extend salvation to the Gentiles as well as the Jews. This was a radical concept to any Jew, including Peter. The Jews thought that they were better than the Gentiles just because they were Jewish. They thought that they were way up high on the ladder, and everyone else was way down at the bottom of the ladder. They had "respect of persons" to their own kind, the Jews. Peter, when he learned better, said, *"Of a truth I perceive that God is no respecter of persons!"* In other words, Peter realized that as far as God was concerned, the ground at the cross is perfectly level, no race stands above or below another.

Now bring that thought back with you to the book of James. James had the same thing in mind. He was scolding the Jewish believers for regarding one group of people as being better, more special than a different group. They had a foul mixture of salvation and prejudice that is never appropriate for a child of God. And in this case, we will find that their preferential treatment did not have to do with **race**, it had to do with **riches**.

A faulty comparison

James 2:2 *For if there come unto your assembly a man with a gold ring, in goodly apparel, and there come in also a poor man in vile raiment; 3 And ye have respect to him that weareth the gay clothing, and say unto him, Sit thou here in a good place; and say to the poor, Stand thou there, or sit here under my footstool: 4 Are ye not then partial in yourselves, and are become judges of evil thoughts?*

Verses two through four make up one long sentence, one continuous thought. James was painting a picture for them of what was going on in their churches. I am not certain how he knew; maybe God told him, or maybe word came from someone who had seen it personally, but either way, the picture he painted was an ugly one. Somewhere along the line, these scattered Jewish believers had begun to compare people on externals and had begun to treat them very differently based on those externals. They had begun to cater to those who were wealthy and be rude to those who were not.

61

James asked them a question that went something like this:

"If you fine folks are in church one day, and you see a visitor come in, and that visitor is wearing really fine, expensive clothes, gold rings dripping off of his fingers, money oozing out of his pockets, and then you see another visitor come in behind him, a guy in nasty worn-out clothes, a guy who is obviously so poor that he can't afford to pay attention, and if you then roll out the red carpet for the rich guy and treat the poor guy like he has some communicable disease, aren't you demonstrating partiality, and isn't your decision making process evil?"

You see, by making a comparison of people based on their wealth, they were using an entirely different standard of measurement than God uses. Since when has God ever shown favoritism to people simply because they have money? How foolish to even think such a thing!

Are there measures of comparison that God uses? Yes, there are in fact. Let me show you one:

Matthew 25:14 *For the kingdom of heaven is as a man travelling into a far country, who called his own servants, and delivered unto them his goods. 15 And unto one he gave five talents, to another two, and to another one; to every man according to his several ability; and straightway took his journey. 16 Then he that had received the five talents went and traded with the same, and made them other five talents. 17 And likewise he that had received two, he also gained other two. 18 But he that had received one went and digged in the earth, and hid his lord's money. 19 After a long time the lord of those servants cometh, and reckoneth with them. 20 And so he that had received five talents came and brought other five talents, saying, Lord, thou deliveredst unto me five talents: behold, I have gained beside them five talents more. 21 His lord said unto him, Well done, thou **good** and **faithful** servant: thou hast been **faithful** over a few things, I will make thee ruler over many things: enter thou into the joy of thy lord. 22 He also that had received two talents came and said, Lord, thou deliveredst unto me two talents: behold, I have gained two other talents beside them. 23 His lord said unto him, Well done, **good** and **faithful***

*servant; thou hast been **faithful** over a few things, I will make thee ruler over many things: enter thou into the joy of thy lord.* **24** *Then he which had received the one talent came and said, Lord, I knew thee that thou art an hard man, reaping where thou hast not sown, and gathering where thou hast not strawed:* **25** *And I was afraid, and went and hid thy talent in the earth: lo, there thou hast that is thine.* **26** *His lord answered and said unto him, Thou **wicked** and **slothful** servant, thou knewest that I reap where I sowed not, and gather where I have not strawed:* **27** *Thou oughtest therefore to have put my money to the exchangers, and then at my coming I should have received mine own with usury.* **28** *Take therefore the talent from him, and give it unto him which hath ten talents.* **29** *For unto every one that hath shall be given, and he shall have abundance: but from him that hath not shall be taken away even that which he hath.*

Now please pay attention to the basis on which God compared these three men. It had nothing to do with them having money because none of them had any of their own money, the only money they had in their possession belonged to their master. None of them are recorded as having a dime of their own. So, what then did the master compare them based on? Do you notice those words that were emphasized? The word *good* is used twice, the word *faithful* is found four times, the word *wicked* is used once, and the word *slothful* is found once. Every single one of these terms deals with **character**, not with **possessions**! God compares people based on character, and then He either elevates them or demotes them based on that character. He uses them or sets them aside based on that character. He rewards them or punishes them based on that character.

Now come back to the book of James. Should these local churches that James was writing to have been comparing and evaluating people? The answer is yes! Every church ought to compare and evaluate people. The problem is not with comparing and evaluating, it is with the faulty methodology that they were using to do so.

You say, "Preacher, I don't believe we ought to be comparing and evaluating people at all! That is judging!" Yes, actually, you do. For instance: if your pastor died, and you brought in two men to candidate for the position of pastor, and one of them had been married and divorced seven times and was now living with his boyfriend while beating puppies and producing child pornography and shooting up elementary schools, and the other candidate was not doing any of those things, and was living right in every area, which one would you choose?

You have just made an evaluation and comparison.

If you find yourselves needing another deacon, and you can choose between a man who does not come to church very often and a man who comes to every single service, which one would you choose?

You have just made an evaluation and comparison.

If you are sick and in need of a doctor, would you say, "Oh, it doesn't matter if I go to the guy who got his medical degree from Harvard or the guy who learned medicine by sitting home and watching CSI?"

You have just made an evaluation and comparison.

Jesus had thousands of followers, but He evaluated all of them and selected only twelve to be apostles. It is right and Biblical and logical to evaluate and compare. But what is not right is to do so based on irrelevant things like money rather than on essential things like faithfulness and purity.

My wife has been the church pianist at our church for more than twenty years, and she is very good at it. But during those years there have been at least four other people who were better piano players than she is. But I kept her right in her position. Why? She was always the most faithful of all of them! The others have not been even close to being as dependable as she is. They would skip Sunday School, skip other services, come in late, not show up for practice. Faithfulness matters.

We have had extremely talented singers through the years that we chose not to use, while we had less talented people sing almost every service. Why? Purity. The ones I am thinking of never would live right, and so we made an evaluation and comparison and chose to utilize the ones who were living right.

There is nothing wrong with making comparisons, not now, and not back in the days of James. What was wrong then and is wrong now is when we make comparisons based on faulty criteria. They were doing so, and their faulty comparison was based on money.

Now before we move on, please let me add another thought to this. We should never choose anyone for a position based on money (deacon, treasurer, trustee, whatever) but we should also never **refuse** to choose a person because they have money. Some very wealthy people are also very faithful and pure, and they should not be held back just because they also happen to have money. Simply put, money should not be an issue for us **either way**.

A forceful reminder

James 2:5 *Hearken, my beloved brethren, Hath not God chosen the poor of this world rich in faith, and heirs of the kingdom which he hath promised to them that love him?*

I have to believe that as James was putting pen to paper to write these words, his mind was flashing back to many, many years ago. Do you remember the family that James grew up in? They were poor, so very poor that they had to offer a turtledove, the sacrifice of poverty. James's father was just a carpenter, not a position of wealth. Yet it was into that very family that God chose to place His Son, James's half-brother Jesus. That obviously meant very little to him as a child since he grew to adulthood despising Jesus and trying to get Him killed. But after he got saved, it must have amazed him to think of it. We rejoice that God became flesh and dwelt among us; James could rejoice that God became flesh and dwelt under the same roof with him!

Jesus never shied away from the poor. In fact, Jesus Himself was poor, the Bible tells us in Matthew 8:20 that He did not even have a place to lay His head.

Did some rich people follow Christ? Yes. Joseph of Arimathaea, Nicodemus, Mary, Martha, and Lazarus; there were some people of means that did follow Him. But the bulk of His followers were poor. Most of the people that accepted Him in the years after His death were poor. Even today most of the people that accept Him are either lower class economically or maybe middle class. Some very rich people accept Him, but not many. James was reminding them that if they were to look around among themselves, they might not want to be showing favoritism to the rich, because most of them were not rich!

James 2:6 *But ye have despised the poor. Do not rich men oppress you, and draw you before the judgment seats? 7 Do not they blaspheme that worthy name by the which ye are called?*

That word *despised* is a very strong word. It is the Greek word for honor (*timao*) with a letter at the front (an alpha privative) of it that negates it. It means to insult and to treat with contempt. It is not just that they were extra nice to the rich, they were also "extra not nice" to the poor. But in so doing they forgot something that James did not intend to let them forget. It was rich men that were the cause of them being scattered and persecuted. It was rich men that were capturing and imprisoning and killing them. It was rich men that were actually brazen enough to be out there blaspheming the name of Jesus. If they were going to discriminate based on money, they would have been wiser to roll out the red carpet for the poor and save their contempt for the rich!

And by the way, I would be willing to guess that those folks eventually learned something that every generation of pastors ever since has eventually learned: the fact that someone in the church *has* a lot of money does not necessarily mean they are *giving* a lot of money. Some do, and I thank God for those who allow God to use them in a powerful way; they are an amazing blessing.

But I have seen over and over and over and over that the bulk of the giving will come from those of whom you would least expect it. In the early days of our church, we lost a family that had a lot, and I mean *a lot* of money. When we did another pastor made the statement, "Well, they'll close down now; that was their money that just left." I literally laughed. Out loud. You see, what I knew that he did not know was that I had brand new baby Christians in low paying jobs that were already giving more than that wealthy family was.

By the way, if everyone tithes, from the full-time, job-working adults, to the retirement income seniors, to the part-time working teenagers, to the kids who get allowances and birthday money, the needs of a church will always be met, even if there is not a single rich person among them.

A fulfilling of the Law

James 2:8 *If ye fulfil the royal law according to the scripture, Thou shalt love thy neighbour as thyself, ye do well:* **9** *But if ye have respect to persons, ye commit sin, and are convinced of the law as transgressors.*

I want you to pay attention to that two-word phrase "royal law" that James used. Let me tell you what is unique about it: this is the only place in the entire Bible that it is found. Humanly speaking, among the Biblical writers, James coined this phrase.

James knew "the law." He was a full-blooded Jew; he grew up memorizing and observing the law of Moses every day of his life. But in later years as a born-again Christian he, under the inspiration of the Holy Ghost, picked out one part of it (Leviticus 19:18) and called that one part the "royal law." The part of the law that is at the top of the list, in other words.

These scattered persecuted Christians were neglecting to love their neighbors. Their neighbors were the poor, not the rich. These Christians were in a situation much closer to that of the poor than they were to that of the rich. Yet when the rich and the poor showed up for service, they were rolling out the red carpet for the rich and despising the poor.

Now, they would most likely have regarded doing so as a simple matter of preference. But look at verse nine and notice what James regarded it as–sin! Their favoritism of the rich over the poor was quite literally a sin. James told them that they had broken the law and become transgressors because of what they were doing.

Now please understand this. It was true then, and it is true now that many people whom we call poor would really, if we are honest, be more properly classified as lazy.

The most hilarious sight I have recently seen was a guy in town holding up a sign that said, "Hungry, please help." What made it funny is that he was *sitting on a lawnmower!*

That, friends, is just lazy.

That is, in fact, the character flaw that we saw from the third servant in the parable from Matthew 25, the one that Jesus called "wicked and slothful." A church is going to be a magnet for those kinds of people because they figure we are soft-hearted enough just to throw money at them without asking questions. By the way, we are not. We are going to do our best to "compare and evaluate" and then weed out people who are wicked and slothful. For people like that we are going to do our best to roll a carpet right out the back door for them, because I do not want our hard-working folks getting infected with slothfulness, nor do I want the giving of our hard-working people squandered on those who are too lazy to work and just want a handout.

But it was also true then, and it is true now that there are a good many folks who are hard-working, honest, and still poor. Those folks we better be in the habit of helping and loving and rolling out the red carpet for. Those poor saved folks we better love and respect and honor just as much as we would the rich saved folks.

If a church forgets that it is supposed to minister to the poor and outcast of society, that church has strayed far afield from where God intends for it to be.

A man visited our church recently and just fell in love with what we are doing ministering to the homeless and hurting. He and I sat down for a meal and talked for a while, and he told me something that just broke my heart.

A church near to where he lives had an old building across the street that they never used. The county approached them about buying it for a specific purpose. They wanted to renovate it and make it a transition facility for non-violent prisoners who were being released back into society. Not murderers, not rapists, not people who assault others, just people who messed up in a non-violent way, had paid their dues and were being released. They wanted to have a place where they could come for a few weeks till they could find a job and get back on their feet.

A church... a church turned them down because that would "mess up their neighborhood."

Apparently, as a church, we need to be reaching out and winning very good, nice, reputable, respectable sinners, not *actual* sinners.

Yeah. Let's just behave like the rest of the world, or worse. Let's show respect of persons like we are a fortune 500 company looking for CEO material.

God help us. We ought to be rolling out the red carpet, and we should not care whether the feet walking across it are in thousand-dollar Perry Ellis shoes, mud-caked work boots, ratty tennis shoes, or completely bare and covered in a week of dirt.

Chapter Seven
Law In Order

James 2:10 *For whosoever shall keep the whole law, and yet offend in one point, he is guilty of all.* **11** *For he that said, Do not commit adultery, said also, Do not kill. Now if thou commit no adultery, yet if thou kill, thou art become a transgressor of the law.* **12** *So speak ye, and so do, as they that shall be judged by the law of liberty.* **13** *For he shall have judgment without mercy, that hath shewed no mercy; and mercy rejoiceth against judgment.*

In the last chapter, as we examined the first nine verses of chapter two, we learned that the churches to whom James was writing had developed a character flaw. They were showing partiality to the rich and despising the poor. People who showed up in their churches dressed well and with bulging wallets found the red carpet rolled out for them, but people who showed up in rags with not a shekel to their names were made to feel like the scum of the earth. James was fairly hard on them for what they were doing, as he pointed out that they were making evaluations based on the wrong criteria. If anything, in their circumstances, they would have been more logical to show partiality to the poor!

In this section, James will continue speaking along the same lines. But this time he will do so focusing on something that was right in line with his own character, the law. We will call this chapter *Law In Order*.

Perhaps not surprisingly, James mentions the law ten times in these few short chapters. He has already done so three times:

James 1:25 *But whoso looketh into the perfect law of liberty, and continueth therein, he being not a forgetful hearer, but a doer of the work, this man shall be blessed in his deed.*

James 2:8 *If ye fulfil the royal law according to the scripture, Thou shalt love thy neighbour as thyself, ye do well:*

James 2:9 *But if ye have respect to persons, ye commit sin, and are convinced of the law as transgressors.*

In these next four verses, James will mention the law three times. Let's see what he has to say about it.

The composition of the old law

In the previous verse, James had just said this:

James 2:9 *But if ye have respect to persons, ye commit sin, and are convinced of the law as transgressors.*

Since Leviticus 19:18, the royal law, had told them to love their neighbor as themselves, any failure to do so was a sin.

But James knew what his readers would be prone to think at this point:

"Well, we may be violating that one point of the law that we don't like, but that's really no big deal since we are keeping pretty much all of the rest of the law! We probably keep ninety-eight or ninety-nine percent of the law religiously, so our failure in that one point really isn't even worth mentioning..."

Isn't that exactly how people think? Parents, when your kids were at home and you told them to clean their room completely, top to bottom, and they cleaned it all except for a small pile of dirty clothes they left in the corner, what did they say to you when you fussed at them?

You who were bosses at work, when your employees did most of what you said but left out one little part, what did they say when you confronted them?

James knew that is how it would be, so he began this section with these words:

James 2:10 *For whosoever shall keep the whole law, and yet offend in one point, he is guilty of all.*

Let me tell you how remarkable of a statement this was: there were at least 618 recognized laws in the law of Moses. That means that a person who broken only one law had a score of

99.84%. There is pretty much no test you will ever take in life where 99.84% is actually a *failing grade!* But that is exactly what James said to them. He told them that if they break one out of those 618 laws, they were guilty of breaking all!

You say, "Preacher, how is that possible?" That is where the composition of the law comes in. There are two possible ways that we can view the law. One, we can view it as a buffet bar of 618 different items, kind of like a legal Golden Corral... (Oh, I am okay with that "no idol's" thing, and I have no problem with "thou shalt not lie with mankind as with womankind," so I will load up on those. But I think I will just pass on that "thou shalt not commit adultery" thing...)

Or two, we can view it as a chain of 618 links. Let me ask you something. If you are driving down the road hauling a massive piece of equipment, held down by a chain of 618 links, how many chains do you have? One. How many links do you have to break to break the chain? One. That is exactly how James is telling us to think of the law. It is not "a collection of laws," it is "the law."

When a person robs a bank, what do people say of him, "he broke *a law*," or "he broke *the law?*" They say that he broke the law!

What does the law demand, "pretty goodness" or perfection? Perfection! If you break so much as one law, you are a lawbreaker, and you are subject to punishment. The level of punishment will vary based on what you have done, but you are still a lawbreaker. And why is that? Look at the next verse:

James 2:11 *For he that said, Do not commit adultery, said also, Do not kill. Now if thou commit no adultery, yet if thou kill, thou art become a transgressor of the law.*

Notice those first four words, "For he that said." Who exactly was it that said, "Thou shalt not commit adultery?" God.

Who was it that said, "Thou shalt not kill?" God.

Every single Old Testament law was given by God, so how many of them were they expected to keep? All of them!

God expects perfection:

Romans 3:23 *For all have sinned, and come short of the glory of God;*

73

But here is the problem: Peter said that no one was able to keep the law:

Acts 15:6 *And the apostles and elders came together for to consider of this matter.* **7** *And when there had been much disputing, Peter rose up, and said unto them, Men and brethren, ye know how that a good while ago God made choice among us, that the Gentiles by my mouth should hear the word of the gospel, and believe.* **8** *And God, which knoweth the hearts, bare them witness, giving them the Holy Ghost, even as he did unto us;* **9** *And put no difference between us and them, purifying their hearts by faith.* **10** *Now therefore why tempt ye God, to put a yoke upon the neck of the disciples, which neither our fathers nor we were able to bear?*

That is exactly why Christ had to come and do what He did:

Galatians 4:4 *But when the fulness of the time was come, God sent forth his Son, made of a woman, made under the law,* **5** *To redeem them that were under the law, that we might receive the adoption of sons.*

Paul later said this of the law:

Galatians 3:22 *But the scripture hath concluded all under sin, that the promise by faith of Jesus Christ might be given to them that believe.* **23** *But before faith came, we were kept under the law, shut up unto the faith which should afterwards be revealed.* **24** *Wherefore the law was our schoolmaster to bring us unto Christ, that we might be justified by faith.* **25** *But after that faith is come, we are no longer under a schoolmaster.*

The composition of the old law is such that breaking any one part of it breaks all of it, and if you do not keep it perfectly, you are just as guilty as if you had broken everything.

We think of that in terms of salvation. Everyone is guilty; everyone is lost and on their way to hell; everyone has broken God's law.

But remember that James was thinking of it in regard to the particular sin these churches were committing. The fact that we are saved and have been redeemed from being under the law does not change the fact that the law is out there and still needs to be acknowledged. But now, while acknowledging and learning from that old law, we are about to see that we have the blessed benefit of being under a brand-new law.

The compelling of a better law

James 2:12 *So speak ye, and so do, as they that shall be judged by the law of liberty.*

From everything we have learned of the law, it ought to surprise you to see the words law and liberty used together. That is until you realize that James is now speaking of a different law entirely:

Romans 8:2 *For the law of the Spirit of life in Christ Jesus hath made me free from the law of sin and death.*

The better law is the gospel!

Under the law, we "had to do right" and never could quite get it done.

Under the better law, the gospel, Jesus fulfilled all of the demands of the old law and then saved us and gave us a new nature whereby we now actually have the ability to do right!

Please notice we are under "a" law either way. We are no longer under "the law," but we are still under a law:

Romans 6:14 *For sin shall not have dominion over you: for ye are not under the law, but under grace.*

"Woohoo, now we get to live like devils!" Uh, no:

Romans 6:15 *What then? shall we sin, because we are not under the law, but under grace? God forbid.* **16** *Know ye not, that to whom ye yield yourselves servants to obey, his servants ye are to whom ye obey; whether of sin unto death, or of obedience unto righteousness?* **17** *But God be thanked, that ye were the servants of sin, but ye have obeyed from the heart that form of doctrine which was delivered you.*

May I summarize all of that? We used to "have to do right" and now we "get to do right" because of what Christ did for us!

So how does this apply to what James was saying?

One: They should have been treating poor helpless people well because of how well Christ treated us when we were poor and helpless.

Two: One day we will be judged on the basis of whether or not we treated others like Christ treated us.

We cannot accurately claim to be living by the perfect law of liberty if we are not treating others like Christ treated and treats us. The law of liberty does not give you a license to be a jerk; it gives you a responsibility to be a blessing.

The conflict between the two laws

James 2:13 *For he shall have judgment without mercy, that hath shewed no mercy; and mercy rejoiceth against judgment.*

What are we still talking about? The perfect law of liberty, our responsibility to be a blessing.

So, in that context, look at this verse and notice that mercy and judgment are at odds. The two laws are at odds.

Mercy rejoiceth against judgment is a phrase that indicates a superior gloating over a defeated inferior.

What we have is better than what those under the law had. We have mercy, and therefore we are to extend mercy. There was no mercy under the old law; it was cold and rigid and sharp. He in His mercy rejoiced against the judgment we were under. He gave us a new law and extended mercy to us through Christ. He then expects us to turn and do the same to others.

It is not that we who are in Christ are lawless; in fact, the opposite is true. We are very much under a law, only it is a much better law than before. Here it is: God was good to you when you had nothing good to offer Him, so you go and be good to others.

I think back to my childhood, and truthfully, mom and I did not have much at all. But people in love reached out to us because of and in the name of Christ. That made all the difference.

Go thou and do likewise.

Chapter Eight
Pure Plutonium

James 2:14 *What doth it profit, my brethren, though a man say he hath faith, and have not works? can faith save him?* **15** *If a brother or sister be naked, and destitute of daily food,* **16** *And one of you say unto them, Depart in peace, be ye warmed and filled; notwithstanding ye give them not those things which are needful to the body; what doth it profit?* **17** *Even so faith, if it hath not works, is dead, being alone.* **18** *Yea, a man may say, Thou hast faith, and I have works: shew me thy faith without thy works, and I will shew thee my faith by my works.* **19** *Thou believest that there is one God; thou doest well: the devils also believe, and tremble.* **20** *But wilt thou know, O vain man, that faith without works is dead?* **21** *Was not Abraham our father justified by works, when he had offered Isaac his son upon the altar?* **22** *Seest thou how faith wrought with his works, and by works was faith made perfect?* **23** *And the scripture was fulfilled which saith, Abraham believed God, and it was imputed unto him for righteousness: and he was called the Friend of God.* **24** *Ye see then how that by works a man is justified, and not by faith only.* **25** *Likewise also was not Rahab the harlot justified by works, when she had received the messengers, and had sent them out another way?* **26** *For as the body without the spirit is dead, so faith without works is dead also.*

There is an element found in trace amounts in the earth's crust and also produced by nuclear reactors, a little thing called Plutonium. I am sure that you have heard of it. It is in the news quite a bit, actually. There are two types of it spoken of, two "grades" of it. Do you know the two grades of Plutonium commonly spoken of? Reactor grade and weapons grade. Reactor-grade plutonium is excellent for producing power. In fact, one-third of the power produced in a nuclear power plant comes from Plutonium. But if you refine it further, it takes on a bit of a different characteristic and becomes what is called "weapons-grade plutonium." At that point, it is not so much useful for power as it is useful for destruction. Everyone is keeping their eyes on Iran right now because they are refining plutonium, and they are promising the world that they will stop the process at reactor grade. If they do not (and they very likely will not), they will have what they need to make nuclear bombs.

Plutonium can be either the most helpful thing on earth or the most destructive thing on earth depending on how it is handled and treated. It can either power hospitals and generators and street lights and traffic signals and stadium lights and air conditioning so that old people do not die in the heat and refrigerators so that our food does not spoil, or it can destroy entire cities and end tens of millions of lives by raising the temperature to ten thousand degrees Fahrenheit in under one one-thousandths of a second. Plutonium can be very good, or very bad.

You may be wondering why I am beginning this chapter in this manner. Here is why. The text that I have just read is the "pure plutonium" of the New Testament! It can be either very good for us or very bad for us based exclusively on how it is handled! It is either going to be the most helpful passage in the Bible or the most dangerous passage in the Bible based exclusively on how it is handled! That is why I call this chapter *The Pure Plutonium Of Scripture.*

A perplexing question

James 2:14 *What doth it profit, my brethren, though a man say he hath faith, and have not works?* ***can faith save him?***

Get that verse firmly in your mind, and now compare it with this one:

Galatians 2:16 *Knowing that a man is not justified by the works of the law, but by the faith of Jesus Christ, even we have believed in Jesus Christ, that we might be justified by the faith of Christ, and not by the works of the law: for by the works of the law shall no flesh be justified.*

Looking at those two verses side by side, can you see where even a man like Martin Luther might have gotten a bit confused? It seems a lot like Paul is telling us that we are saved by faith apart from works while James is telling us that we cannot be saved by faith alone, we have to have works!

Was there really, though, a contradiction in thinking between Paul and James? Well, let's examine the one life we do know about and see. We do not know much about James when it comes to works. We assume that he did a lot of work for the Lord because he certainly focused on it and demanded it of others! But what about Paul? Was Paul a man that clung to faith but had no works? That is the kind of person that James is describing. Look at the verse again:

James 2:14 *What doth it profit, my brethren, though a man say he hath faith, and have not works? can faith save him?*

Was Paul a man that said he had faith? Yes! But was he a man that had no works? No!

1 Corinthians 15:9 *For I am the least of the apostles, that am not meet to be called an apostle, because I persecuted the church of God.* **10** *But by the grace of God I am what I am: and his grace which was bestowed upon me was not in vain; but **I laboured more abundantly than they all**: yet not I, but the grace of God which was with me.*

I want you to pay attention to this. Paul said that he did more works for God than any of the apostles. Who did that include? James! Was he denigrating James? Certainly not, nor was he denigrating anyone else. He was simply stating the truth. God sent Paul on three epic missionary journeys; God used Paul to write at least thirteen books of the New Testament. God used Paul to start churches all over the known world; God had Paul stand before governors and emperors preaching the gospel. It is simply true that the greatest worker for God among any of the apostles was Paul. The others were certainly no slouches themselves, but Paul was far and away at the top of the heap when it came to good works for God. So then, from the evidence of his life, would Paul have been the kind of man James was thinking of when he spoke of a man that said he had faith but had no works? No. And was there a contradiction in thinking between James and Paul on the subject of faith and works? Well, at least on the fact that a person ought to have both of them, the answer is no again. We can see from the words of James that he believed in both faith and works, and we can see from the life of Paul that he believed in faith and works.

But that still doesn't fully answer James's rather straightforward question. Here is that question again:

James 2:14 *What doth it profit, my brethren, though a man say he hath faith, and have not works? can faith save him?*

This question can actually be answered with a yes or a no, and that is what James expected. So please allow me to answer it. If a man says he has faith but has no works, can faith save him? The answer is "no." And by the way, Paul would have agreed. We will see this more fully as we make our way through the text, but please let me go ahead and summarize it for you right now. If a person says he has faith in God but lives a life with no works to show for it, then whatever kind of faith he has cannot save him because it is not real, genuine, Biblical, saving faith!

If a man has "faith" but not works, then *the type of faith he has* cannot save him. Real faith could save him, but real faith would produce good works!

A powerful illustration

James 2:15 *If a brother or sister be naked, and destitute of daily food,* **16** *And one of you say unto them, Depart in peace, be ye warmed and filled; notwithstanding ye give them not those things which are needful to the body; what doth it profit?*

James just finished asking a question, and now he has asked another one to illustrate his point. So, let's look at and answer his second question. His question was, "If your brother or sister is hungry and naked and comes to you for help, and you look at them and say, 'be warm and have food in your belly,' then you send them on their way, but you didn't actually give them any food or clothing, was there any worth in what you said?" What is the answer? No! There is no worth at all in it! Now look at the obvious tie-in:

James 2:17 *Even so faith, if it hath not works, is dead, being alone.*

Was there anything wrong with saying "be warm and have food in your belly?" No, there is nothing wrong with saying it, you should say it. But you should also back up your words with works. It is the same way with salvation. A so-called faith that is words only with no works is a faith with no worth, it is a dead faith. James did not disagree with Paul, *he was disagreeing with people who were twisting the type of thing that Paul and others said.* Paul said that we are justified by faith not by works, so a bunch of carnal people were saying, "Well okay then, that means we have no more responsibility! Whoohoo, we can live like devils and be stingy and ignore the hurting and hungry and skip church and drink booze, because we have faith!" Not only did James disagree with that, but Paul did too:

Romans 6:1 *What shall we say then? Shall we continue in sin, that grace may abound?* **2** *God forbid. How shall we, that are dead to sin, live any longer therein?*

Any version of "faith" that does not produce in us holiness and good works and generosity and faithfulness is a dead faith and will send us straight to Hell.

A perspective defined

James 2:18a *Yea, a man may say, Thou hast faith, and I have works:*

At this point in the text James does what other preachers and I often do when we are preaching when we say, "Now you're going to say, 'But preacher, what about...'"

James is anticipating the response that people are going to give to what he has just said. He knows that they are going to say that it is possible for one saved man to be a man of works and another saved man to be a man of faith but for them both to be saved men. Commentator Albert Barnes put it this way:

The sense is, "someone might say," or, "to this it might be urged in reply." ...that religion is not always manifested in the same way, or we should not suppose that, because it is not always exhibited in the same form, it does not exist. One man may manifest it in one way, and another in another, and still both have true piety. One may be distinguished for his faith, and another for his works, and both may have real religion. This objection would certainly have some plausibility, and it was important to meet it. It would seem that all religion was not to be manifested in the same way, as all virtue is not; and that it might occur that one man might be particularly eminent for one form of religion, and another for another; as one man may be distinguished for zeal, and another for meekness, and another for integrity, and another for truth, and another for his gifts in prayer, and another for his large-hearted benevolence. (Barnes, 51)

That is a very good sense of what James is saying that others are going to say in response to him. But he has an answer ready for that in the last half of the verse:

James 2:18b *...shew me thy faith without thy works, and I will shew thee my faith by my works.*

This is both brilliant and hilarious! I do not know if James intended to show a great sense of humor here, but it seems that he did so whether he meant to or not. Look at the first part of his answer:

...show me thy faith without thy works...

That is beautiful. It is also hilarious.

Show me your faith without works?

You cannot do it! Dressing like a monk is a work. Putting on a beany prayer cap is a work. Giving is a work. What does faith look like? The answer is, without works it doesn't actually look like anything, because it is invisible!

Then James said, "and I will show thee my faith by my works.

Let me, please, add my own illustration to what James has just said to, I hope, make it even clearer and more vivid in your mind. I want you to picture the wind. What does the wind look like? Nothing! Absolutely nothing. So how do we know when the wind is blowing? We see and feel the effects of it. Picture a beautiful country lane, lined with so many rose bushes that there are rose petals laying all over the ground. Now picture one of those twisty southern winds coming down the lane, spinning and spinning and spinning. What are you going to see that lets you know there is a twisty southern wind coming down the lane? You are going to see rose petals picked up off of the ground and spinning around in the air. The sight and the smell will be the most beautiful thing you have ever seen, like a miniature whirlwind from the throne room of Heaven.

The wind and the rose petals worked together. But understand this: *you could see the rose petals without the wind, but you could never see the wind without the rose petals.* You can see works without faith, but you can never see faith without works. And it is at that very point that we come to the perspective in this passage that clarifies what James is saying compared to what Paul would say. Look at this verse again compared with a verse from the writings of Paul:

James 2:18 *Yea, a man may say, Thou hast faith, and I have works: **shew me** thy faith without thy works, and I will **shew thee** my faith by my works.*

In James 2:18, who is looking, God or man? Man!

Romans 3:20 *Therefore by the deeds of the law there shall no flesh be justified in* his *sight: for by the law is the knowledge of sin.*

In Romans 3:20, who is looking, God or man? God!

This is the one essential thing that Martin Luther missed, the one thing that would have made it all make sense to him. James isn't talking about works justifying us before God; he is talking about works justifying us before man! He was saying that no human is ever going to believe we are saved if we do not have the works to prove it, and they shouldn't! Works do not save us, but getting saved will produce works in us, and people will be able to see them. If they cannot, then the odds are that the reason we have no works is because we actually do not have saving faith either. Real faith that justifies us before God without works will then produce works that justify us before man.

A painful reminder

James 2:19 *Thou believest that there is one God; thou doest well: the devils also believe, and tremble.*

For a second time, James now tells them what they are going to say before they say it. These some-real/some-not-real-Christians were going to get very puffy with him and point to their monotheism as proof that they were not lost. The Jews and Christians stood largely alone among all the peoples of earth in believing in only one God. The rest of the people of earth believed in hundreds, thousands, and even millions of gods in some cases. So James's readers, at least the ones who had no good works to show for their supposed faith, were doubtless going to pat themselves on the back. This was a very big deal. We expect monotheism, but in their day the rest of the world certainly did not.

Can you not just see their big swollen heads at that point? "Ooooh, look at us; we are saved; we are pure; we are important; we are special because we believe there is only one God!" And then can you not see James slipping up beside them, putting his arm around their shoulders and saying "You believe there is only one God? Wow! That's really great! You guys are really something! You remind me of somebody else that believes just like you do!"

And they go "Really? Who?"

And James responds "The devil..."

And he was right! The very devil himself was right there in heaven before the throne room. If there is any monotheist anywhere, it is the devil! The devil did not say he would exalt his throne above the stars of the gods; he said he would exalt his throne above the stars of God. He did not say that he would be like the high ones; he said he would be like The Most High. You will never find anyone more monotheistic than the devil.

What was James's point? Whichever of James's readers were not for real, whichever ones said they had faith but had no works to prove it, would begin to point to their important points of doctrine, their cherished beliefs as proofs that they were saved. But pretty much everything we regard as a fact, the devil does too! We believe in the literal six days of creation, and the devil does too. We believe in the virgin birth of Christ, and the devil does too. We believe that He died on Calvary for our sins, and the devil does too. We believe that He rose again on the third day, and the devil does too. He was there to see all of these things happen; if anybody believes them, he believes them! But is he saved? No! And neither is anyone else who "believes" these things but has a version of "faith" that never produces any works!

James 2:20 *But wilt thou know, O vain man, that faith without works is dead?*

They knew that there was only one God. James asked them if they were willing to know something that should be just as obvious. Faith without works is a dead faith, not a living faith. Faith that does not change your life and lifestyle will not change your eternal destination.

Do you see what James called people who would say otherwise? Vain men. It is from the word *kenos,* and in this passage, it means *empty, having nothing of value inside.*

James is saying plainly the exact same thing that I have said for years. Lots of people make professions of faith; far fewer actually get saved. You will be able to tell based on what their lives become in the months and years to follow. When you see someone who made a profession of faith years ago and yet his life never changed, he lives in the same old sin, still does not come to church faithfully, still curses, still drinks, etc., etc., that person is *kenos,* empty, there is nothing of value inside. This does not contradict Paul's doctrine, it confirms Paul's doctrine:

2 Corinthians 5:17 *Therefore if any man be in Christ, he is a new creature: old things are passed away; behold, all things are become new.*

If we have not become new, then our belief has made us just as good as the devil and just as saved as the devil too.

A past example

James 2:21 *Was not Abraham our father justified by works, when he had offered Isaac his son upon the altar?*

At this point in the text James introduced something that caused another problem for Martin Luther, and once again it was because of something that Paul said that sounds very different:

Romans 4:1 *What shall we say then that Abraham our father, as pertaining to the flesh, hath found?* **2** *For if Abraham were justified by works, he hath whereof to glory; but not before God.* **3** *For what saith the scripture? Abraham believed God, and it was counted unto him for righteousness.*

Do you see the conundrum? Paul said, *"For if Abraham were justified by works, he hath whereof to glory,"* but James said, *"Was not Abraham our father justified by works, when he had offered Isaac, his son, upon the altar?"* Now be honest, not pious. How many of you are actually willing to admit that even though you know in your heart that there are no contradictions in the Bible, this certainly looks like one! To me it looks for all the world like James was writing to disagree with what Paul was teaching and that James might not even have liked Paul! But anyone thinking that would be wrong yet again. Let's examine this and see why.

What action in the life of Abraham did James point to when he said that Abraham was justified by works? Isaac being placed on the altar. Where in the Bible did that happen? Genesis 22. Does anyone know how old Isaac was by this point? He was an adult, not a little boy, most likely in his thirties! Now let's go to Romans 4 where Paul talked about Abraham being justified by faith.

Romans 4:9 *Cometh this blessedness then upon the circumcision only, or upon the uncircumcision also? for we say that faith was reckoned to Abraham for righteousness.* **10** *How was it then reckoned? when he was in circumcision, or in uncircumcision? Not in circumcision, but in uncircumcision.* **11** *And he received the sign of circumcision, a seal of the righteousness of the faith which he had yet being uncircumcised: that he might be the father of all them that believe, though they* *be not circumcised; that righteousness might be imputed unto them also:*

The first thing we find is that Abraham became righteous by faith before God instituted the rite of circumcision. Well, when did that happen?

Genesis 17:1 *And when Abram was ninety years old and nine, the LORD appeared to Abram, and said unto him, I am the Almighty God; walk before me, and be thou perfect. 2 And I will make my covenant between me and thee, and will multiply thee exceedingly. 3 And Abram fell on his face: and God talked with him, saying, 4 As for me, behold, my covenant is with thee, and thou shalt be a father of many nations. 5 Neither shall thy name any more be called Abram, but thy name shall be Abraham; for a father of many nations have I made thee. 6 And I will make thee exceeding fruitful, and I will make nations of thee, and kings shall come out of thee. 7 And I will establish my covenant between me and thee and thy seed after thee in their generations for an everlasting covenant, to be a God unto thee, and to thy seed after thee. 8 And I will give unto thee, and to thy seed after thee, the land wherein thou art a stranger, all the land of Canaan, for an everlasting possession; and I will be their God. 9 And God said unto Abraham, Thou shalt keep my covenant therefore, thou, and thy seed after thee in their generations. 10 This is my covenant, which ye shall keep, between me and you and thy seed after thee; Every man child among you shall be circumcised. 11 And ye shall circumcise the flesh of your foreskin; and it shall be a token of the covenant betwixt me and you. 12 And he that is eight days old shall be circumcised among you, every man child in your generations, he that is born in the house, or bought with money of any stranger, which is not of thy seed. 13 He that is born in thy house, and he that is bought with thy money, must needs be circumcised: and my covenant shall be in your flesh for an everlasting covenant. 14 And the uncircumcised man child whose flesh of his foreskin is not circumcised, that soul shall be cut off from his people; he hath broken my covenant. 15 And God said unto Abraham, As for Sarai thy wife, thou shalt not call her name Sarai, but Sarah shall her name be. 16 And I will bless her, and give thee a son* *also of her: yea, I will bless her, and she shall be a mother of nations; kings of people shall be of her.* **17** *Then Abraham fell upon his face, and laughed, and said in his heart, Shall a child be born unto him that is an hundred years old? and shall Sarah, that is ninety years old, bear?* **18** *And Abraham said unto God, O that Ishmael might live before thee!* **19** *And God said, Sarah thy wife shall bear thee a son indeed; and thou shalt call his name Isaac: and I will establish my covenant with him for an everlasting covenant, and with his seed after him.*

Abraham was given the rite of circumcision before Isaac was ever born, and Paul said that Abraham was made righteous by faith even before that, which was thirty plus years before he put Isaac on that altar! Let's go back to what Paul said and look a little farther:

Romans 4:13 *For the promise, that he should be the heir of the world, was not to Abraham, or to his seed, through the law, but through the righteousness of faith.* **14** *For if they which are of the law be heirs, faith is made void, and the promise made of none effect:* **15** *Because the law worketh wrath: for where no law is, there is no transgression.* **16** *Therefore it is of faith, that it might be by grace; to the end the promise might be sure to all the seed; not to that only which is of the law, but to that also which is of the faith of Abraham; who is the father of us all,* **17** *(As it is written, I have made thee a father of many nations,) before him whom he believed, even God, who quickeneth the dead, and calleth those things which be not as though they were.* **18** *Who against hope believed in hope, that he might become the father of many nations, according to that which was spoken, So shall thy seed be.* **19** *And being not weak in faith, he considered not his own body now dead, when he was about an hundred years old, neither yet the deadness of Sara's womb:* **20** *He staggered not at the promise of God through unbelief; but was strong in faith, giving glory to God;* **21** *And being fully persuaded that, what he had promised, he was able also to perform.*

According to this, we find that Abraham was made righteous by faith when God came to him and promised that He would give him a son in his old age. That was even earlier, much earlier. That we find in Genesis 15, and in that chapter, Abraham is no more than eighty-five years old because the next thing we see in chapter sixteen is him having Ishmael at age eighty-six. Look at that passage:

Genesis 15:1 *After these things the word of the LORD came unto Abram in a vision, saying, Fear not, Abram: I am thy shield, and thy exceeding great reward. 2 And Abram said, Lord GOD, what wilt thou give me, seeing I go childless, and the steward of my house is this Eliezer of Damascus? 3 And Abram said, Behold, to me thou hast given no seed: and, lo, one born in my house is mine heir. 4 And, behold, the word of the LORD came unto him, saying, This shall not be thine heir; but he that shall come forth out of thine own bowels shall be thine heir. 5 And he brought him forth abroad, and said, Look now toward heaven, and tell the stars, if thou be able to number them: and he said unto him, So shall thy seed be. 6 And he believed in the LORD; and he counted it to him for righteousness.*

This is the exact verse that Paul quoted so many years later:

Romans 4:3 *For what saith the scripture? Abraham believed God, and it was counted unto him for righteousness.*

So according to Paul, Abraham believed God, and that faith in God, apart from works, justified him. And that happened when Abraham was no more than eighty-five years old. That was, bare minimum, fifteen years before Isaac was born and most likely forty-five years minimum before he offered Isaac on Mount Moriah. So according to Paul, Abraham was justified by faith without works forty-five years or so before what James is talking about when he says that Abraham was justified by works as well as by faith. So do you know the one thing we already can conclusively say? James and Paul were not even talking about the same thing! Do you know the second thing we can conclusively say? James never contradicted anything that Paul did say about Abraham. James never even mentioned Abraham believing that he would have a son, or the circumcision, all of that James left out. And the opposite is true as well. Paul never mentioned what James was talking about, the episode on Mount Moriah. The only thing those two spoke about in common was

Abraham being justified. You say, "But preacher, that still doesn't explain the fact that Paul said he was justified by faith without works, and James said that he was justified by works." Which one was right, James or Paul? The answer is "Yes." Yes, Paul was right, and yes, James was right. Since they were speaking of two different events, they were obviously speaking of two different things. As we saw just a few moments ago, the difference is one of perspective. James was not contradicting Paul's doctrine, he was yet again complimenting or completing it. Nothing he said would have gotten the first disagreement from Paul.

When it came to God's perspective, what we would call salvation, Abraham was justified by faith alone when he believed God in his heart when God said the old man would have a child. But does man has the ability to see that belief? No. Once again, what exactly does "belief" look like? You can't see the wind coming down the lane, but you can see the rose petals swirling in it. When Abraham took Isaac up to that mountain, that is something that could be seen. The servants saw them go up there. Isaac saw his father raise the knife. Every generation since has read about it. That work justifies him in our sight. It was the visible proof of inward belief.

Think about it. If Abraham had not believed God, would he have been willing to do what he did? No! Look how firmly he believed him:

Hebrews 11:17 *By faith Abraham, when he was tried, offered up Isaac: and he that had received the promises offered up his only begotten son,* **18** *Of whom it was said, That in Isaac shall thy seed be called:* **19** *Accounting that God was able to raise him up, even from the dead; from whence also he received him in a figure.*

Abraham took Isaac up on that mountain to sacrifice him because he believed that God was going to raise him from the dead! You see, God had already promised that Isaac would be the chosen seed, so Abraham just put two and two together and came to the conclusion that the only way he could sacrifice Isaac and Isaac still be the chosen seed was for God to resurrect him. Now that obviously is not what God planned, but the truth does not change. Abraham believed God, and that justified him in God's sight; Abraham did a work that proved he had believed God and that justifies him in our sight. God was able to see the belief; we are able to see the work. If there is real belief, there will be real works!

James 2:22 *Seest thou how faith wrought with his works, and by works was faith made perfect?* **23** *And the scripture was fulfilled which saith, Abraham believed God, and it was imputed unto him for righteousness: and he was called the Friend of God.*

That word perfect is the word *telos,* and it means *complete.* Faith will save before there is ever the first work done, you can think of the thief on the cross and realize that. But faith is never *complete* until a person who says he believes shows the works that prove he has believed. God did not save us just to save us:

Romans 8:29 *For whom he did foreknow, he also did predestinate to be conformed to the image of his Son, that he might be the firstborn among many brethren.*

God saved us to make us like His Son. We are completely **saved** the moment we truly believe, but we are not truly **complete** until that faith produces visible works in our lives that shows others that we are saved.

Notice that at the end of verse twenty-three James quotes an Old Testament passage that Paul had not quoted. He referred to Abraham being called the friend of God. That is a quote from Isaiah 41:8:

Isaiah 41:8 *But thou, Israel, art my servant, Jacob whom I have chosen, the seed of Abraham my friend.*

Do you know what that does for us? It gives us another way to explain what James and Paul were saying. You will be a *son of God* the moment you believe before you ever do the first work. But sons are not always "friends" to their father, now are they (think of the prodigal son)! But when you obey God by doing the good works that prove that you are saved, at that point you are a friend of God. Paul and James were dealing with two different things. Paul was writing to tell people that they needed to stop trusting in their works to get them to Heaven. James was writing to people to tell them that if they are going to heaven,

91

they need to prove it by their good works! Paul was writing to people who thought they could work their way to heaven. James was writing to people who thought that since they were going to heaven, they did not have to work anymore! Paul was writing to people who needed to be taught how to become sons of God, James was writing to people who needed to be taught how to become friends of God!

James 2:24 *Ye see then how that by works a man is justified, and not by faith only.* **25** *Likewise also was not Rahab the harlot justified by works, when she had received the messengers, and had sent them out another way?* **26** *For as the body without the spirit is dead, so faith without works is dead also.*

The body and the spirit are two different things. Faith and works are two different things. But just like separating the body and the spirit produces death, so does separating faith and works. Faith always comes first, and it is faith that does the saving, apart from works. But if you really have been saved by faith, it will... not might, it WILL produce the works that prove it!

You see now why this passage is the *Pure Plutonium* of Scripture. If it is misunderstood it becomes a weapon that teaches a works salvation and destroys people and sends them to hell. If it is understood it takes people who claim to be saved but are lost and smacks them in the face with the proof that they are lost, namely the fact that their works are the works of a lost person, not the works of a saved person. And it will also serve as a reminder to Christians who are slacking off that their salvation testimony will not mean squat to the lost unless their lives match their testimonies. Powerful...powerful... powerful.

Chapter Nine
The Worst Member of the Church

James 3:1 *My brethren, be not many masters, knowing that we shall receive the greater condemnation.* **2** *For in many things we offend all. If any man offend not in word, the same is a perfect man, and able also to bridle the whole body.* **3** *Behold, we put bits in the horses' mouths, that they may obey us; and we turn about their whole body.* **4** *Behold also the ships, which though they be so great, and are driven of fierce winds, yet are they turned about with a very small helm, whithersoever the governor listeth.* **5** *Even so the tongue is a little member, and boasteth great things. Behold, how great a matter a little fire kindleth!* **6** *And the tongue is a fire, a world of iniquity: so is the tongue among our **members**, that it defileth the whole body, and setteth on fire the course of nature; and it is set on fire of hell.* **7** *For every kind of beasts, and of birds, and of serpents, and of things in the sea, is tamed, and hath been tamed of mankind:* **8** *But the tongue can no man tame; it is an unruly evil, full of deadly poison.* **9** *Therewith bless we God, even the Father; and therewith curse we men, which are made after the similitude of God.* **10** *Out of the same mouth proceedeth blessing and cursing. My brethren, these things ought not so to be.* **11** *Doth a fountain send forth at the same place sweet water and bitter?* **12** *Can the fig tree, my brethren, bear olive berries? either a vine, figs? so can no fountain both yield salt water and fresh.*

In chapter two, James dealt with faith and works.

As chapter three begins he makes a stark transition, and this chapter will deal with the worst member of every church–the tongue.

A warning about leadership

James 3:1 *My brethren, be not many masters, knowing that we shall receive the greater condemnation.* **2a** *For in many things we offend all.*

Masters is from the word *didaskolos.* It means teachers or spiritual leaders. James was dealing with the church about a situation that we often see today: a whole lot more people being preachers than really should be preachers.

I think of professional athletes claiming they are called to preach, yet waiting until their fifteen-year, hundred-million-dollar career is over before actually going into the ministry. Mind you, I am very glad for men who use their platform to speak of Christ. But if God actually calls you to preach, you do not wait until you have made your millions and can no longer run and jump and throw. If you do, I question whether He has called you:

Matthew 4:18 *And Jesus, walking by the sea of Galilee, saw two brethren, Simon called Peter, and Andrew his brother, casting a net into the sea: for they were fishers.* **19** *And he saith unto them, Follow me, and I will make you fishers of men.* **20** *And they straightway left their nets, and followed him.* **21** *And going on from thence, he saw other two brethren, James the son of Zebedee, and John his brother, in a ship with Zebedee their father, mending their nets; and he called them.* **22** *And they immediately left the ship and their father, and followed him.*

Not just athletes, though, also random men in the church who are convinced they are called, but when you ask everyone else, it is clear they are not.

Also, men who cannot do anything else, so they are sure they must be called to ministry.

In the book, "Lectures to My Students," Charles Spurgeon said:

"One brother have I encountered – one

did I say? I have met 10, 20, 100 brethren, who have pleaded that they were sure, quite sure that they were called to the ministry – they were quite certain of it, because they had failed in everything else."

He went on to say:

"The ministry needs the very best of men, and not those who cannot do anything else. A man who would succeed as a preacher would probably do right well either as a grocer, or lawyer, or anything else. A really valuable minister would have excelled at anything." (Spurgeon, 37-38)

Let me say it again: there are a lot more people who are preachers than who actually should be preachers.

This often results in church splits–a discredit to the ministry–and James mentions one more reason why it should not happen:

knowing that we shall receive the greater condemnation...

Preachers will be judged far more strictly than anyone else:

Luke 12:48 *But he that knew not, and did commit things worthy of stripes, shall be beaten with few stripes. For unto whomsoever much is given, of him shall be much required: and to whom men have committed much, of him they will ask the more.*

Think through Scripture. Men that God placed in positions of authority were not allowed to get by with much at all. Moses striking the rock, David and Bathsheba, Korah.

A person better never go into the ministry unless God calls him.

This is one of the reasons why, when a young man comes to me and says, "Preacher, I think God may be calling me to preach," I usually do not even change the look on my face. I do not jump up and down celebrating, and I do not immediately put them in the pulpit. What I usually do is say, "Well, if He is, you will still feel this way next week and next month and the month after that. So, let's just give it some time and find out if this is just an emotional moment for you, or if God is actually calling you."

You see, the ministry is the hardest life on earth. You bear your discouragements and also the discouragements of every single member in your church and all of their family members. You face times where you do right and get ripped to shreds over it. You face times where you stand for right and have very few people if any at all standing with you.

If a person goes into the ministry from the church I pastor, I want to make very sure that it was not just an emotional decision during an emotional moment. I want to make sure he is actually called of God. If he is, he will not shake that feeling tomorrow or next week or the next month.

Conservatively speaking, ninety percent of the people that I have ever personally known that said they were called to preach and went into the ministry have completely bombed and dropped out, and now are not doing anything of the sort.

That tells me that many of them were not called to begin with. It is the fact of one's calling, the unshakable certainty that God Himself put you in that position, that helps the God called preachers to make it through all the hard times.

I want men called to preach out of my church. I want us to send out missionaries and church planters. But I want it to be God that has called them, not just us thinking that they are called and sending them. You see, when we send them out, I do not want them having to come back. I want them able to dig in and continue in the ministry through all the hard times.

Yes, I understand that sometimes people get broken in the ministry and need to come back and heal up. But when ninety percent of the people that say they are called go out and then do not make it, something is going wrong, and the most logical assumption is that not nearly as many people are called as think they have been called.

Notice that James also added this:

For in many things we offend all.

James understood something. Anyone who is in a position of authority and makes his living by speaking is bound to blow it a great many times, even those who actually are legitimately called to the ministry.

And that thought allowed James to segue into the next thought.

A word about the tongue

James 3:2 *For in many things we offend all. If any man offend not in word, the same is a perfect man, and able also to bridle the whole body.*

In other words, everyone, preacher or not, is in the same boat on this one.

James 3:3 *Behold, we put bits in the horses' mouths, that they may obey us; and we turn about their whole body.* **4** *Behold also the ships, which though they be so great, and are driven of fierce winds, yet are they turned about with a very small helm, whithersoever the governor listeth.* **5** *Even so the tongue is a little member, and boasteth great things.*

A tiny little bit controls a mighty horse.

A tiny rudder controls a huge ship.

And a tiny tongue manages to control the entire body, rather than vice versa!

...Behold, how great a matter a little fire kindleth!

Take one tiny little fire, and you have something capable of destroying tens of thousands of acres and taking multiple lives. This is like the tongue!

James 3:6 *And the tongue is a fire, a world of iniquity: so is the tongue among our members, that it defileth the whole body, and setteth on fire the course of nature; and it is set on fire of hell.*

Notice that three times fire is mentioned in reference to the tongue.

The course of nature means "the entire course of your natural life." From young to old the tongue is a problem!

The fact that it is "set on fire of Hell," means that it is supernaturally destructive, as if the devil himself was in it.

If you have lived long enough, you have probably seen instances in which someone wagged their tongue and did as much damage as if a bomb had gone off. That is the kind of evil power James is describing.

James 3:7 *For every kind of beasts, and of birds, and of serpents, and of things in the sea, is tamed, and hath been tamed of mankind:* **8** *But the tongue can no man tame; it is an unruly evil, full of deadly poison.*

This all sounds hopeless. But the point is not to make us hopeless. The point is to make us careful! Careful about every personal conversation, careful about every phone call, careful about every text, especially careful about every group text, careful about every tweet, careful about every snap, careful about every post, careful about every way in which we communicate. The day we get careless with our tongue, disaster will strike.

James 3:9 *Therewith bless we God, even the Father; and therewith curse we men, which are made after the similitude of God.* **10** *Out of the same mouth proceedeth blessing and cursing. My brethren, these things ought not so to be.*

This would hit home with James's readers: scattered Jewish Christians, proud and haughty, yet still convinced that just because of their descent from Abraham they were better than everybody else. No, every human being is made in the image of God. And if we are guilty of blessing God and cursing men, then God really does not think too highly of our blessing. James said, "These things ought not so to be." We Christians ought to never be guilty of talking piously out of a potty mouth.

And by the way, anyone who gets caught uttering several strings of profanities and then uses the excuse, "Well, Peter cursed too," needs to have a meteor dropped on his head. Yes, Peter cursed. But you never did hear Peter say, "Well, David committed adultery and look at how God used him!"

No, when Peter cursed and denied Christ, he went out and wept bitterly. He never did try to justify what he had done by pointing to the wrong that someone else had done.

James 3:11 *Doth a fountain send forth at the same place sweet water and bitter?* **12** *Can the fig tree, my brethren, bear olive berries? either a vine, figs? so can no fountain both yield salt water and fresh.*

Here, James gives four illustrations with one point. Our mouths should be consistent and consistently right.

I think we do not take this nearly seriously enough.

Here is a news story from USA Magazine, in the Shelby Star of January 14, 2007:

> With his lip rings and tattoos, Jay Bakker, son of fallen 80's televangelists Jim and Tammy Bakker - has gone from black sheep to feeding the sheep of his Revolution Church, which he leads in a bar in Brooklyn. "I'm trying to be a pastor who loves people," says Bakker, 31, who looks more like he should be touring with a heavy metal band. "I feel like I've been successful in helping people understand that God loves them the way they are." He's now appearing on the Sundance channel in a six-part series, "One Punk Under God," chronicling the challenge of running an alternative ministry. "It seems like the media wants to say, 'You're a punk-rock preacher.' But if I pull anything from punk, it's loyalty and friendship," Bakker says. "I might seem like a punk because **I may cuss every now and then**, but I wouldn't seem like a punk to most punks."

There is obviously so much in there that is so wrong. But just in the context of what we have been talking about, notice how he minimizes the fact that he "cusses every now and then."

Look at what Jesus said:

Matthew 12:36 *But I say unto you, That every idle word that men shall speak, they shall give account thereof in the day of judgment.*

Jesus meant this when He said it. Do not ever give yourself a pass on filthy talk. There ought to be a whole lot of Christians around the altar on a regular basis apologizing to the Lord for the things that come out of their mouths and begging Him for forgiveness and for the help to never speak a word that is disgraceful to God ever again.

Chapter Ten
What Kind of Wisdom?

James 3:13 *Who is a wise man and endued with knowledge among you? let him shew out of a good conversation his works with meekness of wisdom.* **14** *But if ye have bitter envying and strife in your hearts, glory not, and lie not against the truth.* **15** *This wisdom descendeth not from above, but is earthly, sensual, devilish.* **16** *For where envying and strife is, there is confusion and every evil work.* **17** *But the wisdom that is from above is first pure, then peaceable, gentle, and easy to be intreated, full of mercy and good fruits, without partiality, and without hypocrisy.* **18** *And the fruit of righteousness is sown in peace of them that make peace.*

In 1937, architect Frank Lloyd Wright built a house for industrialist Hibbard Johnson. One rainy evening, Johnson was entertaining distinguished guests for dinner when the roof began to leak. The water seeped through directly above Johnson himself, dripping steadily onto his bald head. Irate, he called Wright in Phoenix, Arizona. "Frank," he said, "you built this beautiful house for me, and we enjoy it very much. But I have told you the roof leaks, and right now I am with some friends and distinguished guests, and it is leaking right on top of my head." Wright's reply was heard by all of the guests. "Well, Hib, why don't you move your chair?" (Today, 1).

Wisdom is not knowing that the roof is leaking on your head and calling someone to complain; wisdom is moving your chair.

James just finished talking about the tongue. Now he is going to deal with wisdom, which will either make our tongue and everything else about us helpful or harmful depending on which kind of "wisdom" it is.

An important question

James 3:13 *Who is a wise man and endued with knowledge among you? let him shew out of a good conversation his works with meekness of wisdom.*

James knew he was writing to a mixed crowd in every which way. Some saved, some lost, some spiritual, some carnal.

He asked a question knowing that not all can <u>rightfully</u> say "me," but knowing that everyone will do so anyway.

Look at that question and think of how we would ask it. (Who is a wise man, or even a wise woman among you?)

Think of how everyone would instinctively have responded.

James then placed a qualifier on it, a proof of who actually is what that first phrase says:

...let him shew out of a good conversation his works with meekness of wisdom.

Conversation. When we think of that word, to us it means "having a talk." But when you see that word in the Bible, it means much more than a conversation; it means **works** as well as **words**. It means "your entire manner of living."

Do you remember that old children's song that said it so perfectly? "Your talk talks and your walk talks but your walk talks louder than your talk talks."

James begins here to describe real wisdom, meekness of wisdom; wisdom that is peaceful and thoughtful rather than proud and boisterous, thought-provoking wisdom rather than "picket line wisdom" or "political activist wisdom."

These college professors around our country like the lady in California who used a bunch of filthy four-letter words to express how happy she was that Barbara Bush died? I do not know what kind of intelligence she has; she may have a very high IQ for all I know, but I do know beyond any doubt that she has no wisdom at all and should never be entrusted as a teacher over any precious young person.

I know more than one preacher who uses vulgarity from the pulpit, insults women, and makes racist comments. These men are booked up for years in advance with people wanting them to come preach. What people are doing is inviting men into their pulpit who have absolutely no wisdom whatsoever.

Real wisdom turns a person into a gentleman or a lady, not a jerk.

An identifying truth

James 3:14 *But if ye have bitter envying and strife in your hearts, glory not, and lie not against the truth.*

Again, James knew that everyone would answer "me" to his question.

He also knew that some of them needed to be made aware of the fact that they were lying to themselves. People do that, a lot. Like the man who is incredibly proud of himself for still wearing the same size jeans he wore in high school. It is not too hard to do that as long as you let that big gigantic gut of yours lap over your belt like you just swallowed a one hundred-pound sack of potatoes.

People are in the habit of lying to themselves. So James, knowing this, said:

But if ye have bitter envying and strife in your hearts, glory not, and lie not against the truth.

In other words, "Don't tell me you have this godly kind of wisdom if at the same time you have bitter envying and strife in your hearts. Stop lying against the truth."

Now we should say a few things about that phrase, "Bitter envying." In other words, just like lust can be either good or bad, so can envy. Envy can be either bitter or sweet.

You can either envy each other in a way which leads you to tear each other down, or you can envy each other in a way that makes you want to emulate the good that you see in each other.

I envy some people's even temperament; I want to emulate what I see in them.

By contrast, bitter envying is not the type of envying that makes you want to be better yourself; it is the type of envying that makes you want to act in a destructive way toward others, to gossip about them and tear them down, to undermine them and hurt their efforts.

If you are marked by the bitter kind of envy, then the word from James to you is to *glory not, and lie not against the truth*; you are not actually wise, no matter how much you claim that you are.

An insight on wisdom

James 3:15 *This wisdom descendeth not from above, but is earthly, sensual, devilish.*

We have seen already in James that lust can be either good or bad... envy can be either good or bad... and now we see that wisdom can also be either good or bad! What is wisdom? It is knowing how to apply knowledge. Knowledge is "striking a match can start a fire." Wisdom is "striking a match can start a fire, and if I start a fire in a fireplace, I will both stay safe and get warm."

But, surprisingly, wisdom is also, "striking a match can start a fire; if I start a fire in an abandoned building, I get the kick of getting to watch it burn down."

Wisdom can descend from above, or wisdom can come from beneath, from that which is earthly and sensual and devilish.

Wisdom can come from above, but the kind of "wisdom" that leads you to tear others down is from a far different source.

James mentions three sources for it:

Earthly: from "the world." (Hollywood, politics, academia, social media)

Sensual: from the passions of man. (It is inherent in our fallen nature)

Devilish: from the devil (He is constantly seeking to get us to see things his way)

Do you see why this kind of so-called wisdom is actually so devilish and dangerous? Look at what James says next that shows the results of it:

James 3:16 *For where envying and strife is, there is confusion and every evil work.*

Where there is that "bitter envy," that "tearing down" of others, there will be a couple of other things:

Confusion:

A pastor I know had been at a church for a very long time. He had lived right, been faithful to his wife and family, and done right. Then, out of the blue, a rumor got started that he had been unfaithful to his wife. It nearly destroyed his entire life.

About a year later his wife ended up with cancer, and it was in its final stages before they realized it, and very aggressive. Within weeks she was on her deathbed. The day that she died, her husband was standing there by her bedside holding her hand, and she looked up at him and said, "I have something I need to tell you before I go."

He said, "What is it, honey?"

She said, "Well, I never did tell you this, but for a long time I was really very jealous of how much time and effort you put into the church. So, I tried to find some way to make it to where you would spend less time with the church and more time with me. I don't like to tell you this, but I am the one that started the rumor that you were unfaithful."

What did James say? *For where envying and strife is, there is confusion.* That husband and pastor spent more than a year confused beyond measure trying to find out who would say such a horrible thing about him, then faced an even deeper confusion when he realized it was his own beloved bride that had done it. She got envious, and that envying and strife, that sensual, earthly, devilish wisdom produced confusion.

He also said it produces "every evil work." You will notice that statement is very broad! It is intended to be so. It is James way of saying that nothing is regarded as "off limits" to a person who gets jealous and desires to tear someone else down.

A person eaten up with jealousy does not have any boundaries. That person will do anything in their quest for destruction.

That is some horrible, horrible wisdom! It is wisdom that has been twisted and perverted and birthed out of hell itself. But there is another kind of wisdom:

James 3:17 *But the wisdom that is from above is first pure, then peaceable, gentle, and easy to be intreated, full of mercy and good fruits, without partiality, and without hypocrisy.*

Here is the second kind of wisdom, the good kind.

Notice that although this kind of wisdom is many things, James says that it is **first** pure. **Any so-called wisdom that results in impurity rather than purity is not wisdom from above.**

I do not care if that kind of "wisdom" comes equipped with four Ph.D.'s and a tenured salary, it is devilish, not heavenly.

After pure we find that it is peaceable, gentle, and easy to be intreated. These three go together.

Several years ago, I received a phone call from a preacher that I did not know personally, only by name. He said, "Brother Wagner, I have an issue that I need to discuss with you. I want you to know that before I called you, I called Brother So-and-So and asked him one question: 'Is Brother Wagner a reasonable man?' Brother so-and-so said that you were. That is why I am taking the chance to call you."

He then laid out the reasons for his call, some things he had heard about me and a mission work that I was associated with. We talked for probably forty-five minutes, and it was a levelheaded, honest conversation, with both sides being completely easy to speak to.

By the way, not only did we get the issue resolved, he and I became friends that day, and are extremely good friends to this very day. Wisdom is peaceable, gentle, easy to be intreated.

We then read that it is "full of mercy and good fruits." These two go together. They describe someone who is merciful and kind. Real heavenly wisdom makes a person just like that. Real wisdom is not vindictive.

106

Years ago, a lady showed up at the church and asked to speak to Dana and me afterward. She had just gotten to the area; she and her husband had split up, but she knew the relationship needed to be restored and wondered if we would be willing to help. I assured her that we would. So, with her sitting there in the office along with Dana and me, I called her husband. I introduced myself, told him that my wife and I were sitting here with his wife and that she had expressed a desire for reconciliation. I told him that we would be willing to drive to where he was, pay all of our own expenses, and sit down and talk with him and his wife together and help them make things right with each other.

To be very kind, the best way I can describe this guy is "ignorant, redneck, south end of a northbound mule kind of person." Mr. Genius said, "I'll talk to her when she comes crawling back like the low-down dog she is!"

That is some low-level wisdom right there, isn't it? His wife has now moved on with another man, and the last time I heard, he was still a lonely hick loser.

Moving on through the verse, we find that heavenly wisdom is "without partiality." That means "not showing unjust favoritism or unjust antagonism."

Preachers, by the way, can be some of the worst at this, blasting other preachers they do not like for something they do, then giving those they do like a pass on the same thing or something worse. But everyday church folks often do the same, demanding that the ax fall hard and heavy on someone who has done wrong, and then changing their tune completely when a member of their friend or family circle does the same thing.

Real wisdom, heavenly wisdom, is not like that. It is without partiality. It knows how to say, "That Democrat was wicked for what he did," and it also knows how to say, "So was that Republican" for the exact same thing. It knows how to say, "That person's boy or girl should not have acted that way," and it also knows how to say, "My boy or girl should not have acted that way."

Then we find that real wisdom is "without hypocrisy." In other words, real wisdom, heavenly wisdom, is demonstrated by actually being who you seem to be.

Years ago, we dealt with a young lady who was constantly getting involved in one horrible sin after another. Each time it happened, her parents came to me greatly concerned that no one think badly of their daughter. They had no concern whatsoever about the fact that their daughter was living the life of a little devil, no, they just wanted to make sure that no one thought she was living the life of a little devil.

Needless to say, they managed to raise a full-fledged, card-carrying, grade A, USDA choice hypocrite.

There is wisdom from above, and there is wisdom from beneath. Heavenly wisdom is pure, peaceable, gentle, easy to be intreated, full of mercy and good fruits, without partiality, and without hypocrisy. Wisdom from beneath, devilish wisdom, produces all of the exact opposites.

An insightful analogy

James 3:18 *And the fruit of righteousness is sown in peace of them that make peace.*

As James gets into verse eighteen, he begins to use an illustration, an agricultural illustration. He uses the word "sown," referring to how a farmer puts seeds into the ground.

He says *the fruit of righteousness is sown in peace of them that make peace.* Please allow me to paraphrase that so that you will know what James was driving at.

The wise farmer does not stir up a tempest and then sow seeds. He does not run a herd of ten thousand buffalo through his field, choking the sky with dust, and then try to sow seeds in the midst of all that turmoil.

The wise Christian does not do that either. The truth we tell may stir things up, but a wise Christian will not stir things up for the sake of stirring things up and then call it "witnessing." Being a rabble-rouser is not the same thing as being a seed sower.

I am witnessing to a gentleman these days, and there are a great many things he is just wrong about. And yet I am not even arguing with him on any of those things. Do you know why? Because he is not saved yet. My goal is not to get him thinking right on ten thousand issues and then get him saved; that will simply never happen. My goal is to get him saved so that he can begin thinking right on the ten thousand issues.

Not just for preachers but for everyone, there really are two kinds of wisdom. If you take the knowledge that God has given you and then do harm and damage to the cause of Christ with it, I do not care if your IQ makes Einstein look dumb; you do not have real heavenly wisdom.

If you have real heavenly wisdom, you will take the knowledge that God has given you and behave in such a way that your very lifestyle brings glory and honor to Christ who gave you that wisdom. If you have real heavenly wisdom, you will live in such a way that the lost are drawn to you so that they can be drawn to Christ who saved you.

Yes, wisdom tells the truth, and yes, the truth is very often divisive and unpopular. I am not telling you to avoid the truth. I am telling you that the way you tell the truth and more importantly the way you live the truth ought to be making the truth itself attractive because the God who gave that truth is attractive.

So, what kind of wisdom do you have?

Chapter Eleven
Inward, Christian Soldiers

James 4:1 From whence come wars and fightings among you? come they not hence, even of your lusts that war in your members? 2 Ye lust, and have not: ye kill, and desire to have, and cannot obtain: ye fight and war, yet ye have not, because ye ask not. 3 Ye ask, and receive not, because ye ask amiss, that ye may consume it upon your lusts. 4 Ye adulterers and adulteresses, know ye not that the friendship of the world is enmity with God? whosoever therefore will be a friend of the world is the enemy of God. 5 Do ye think that the scripture saith in vain, The spirit that dwelleth in us lusteth to envy? 6 But he giveth more grace. Wherefore he saith, God resisteth the proud, but giveth grace unto the humble. 7 Submit yourselves therefore to God. Resist the devil, and he will flee from you.

James has already dealt with many things that surely made his readers wince in pain a bit. But if you thought he had been hard on them thus far, I can assure you that what he is about to say will make all previous material seem like a fuzzy pink love letter. James is about to drop the hammer and even call people some unkind names! And, please, bear in mind that he will say every single word under the inspiration of the Holy Ghost! It is James doing the writing in his own unique style, but it is still God Himself dictating the material. With that in mind let's cover this section of verses which we will call *Inward Christian Soldiers.*

111

In 1865 a man named Sabine Baring Gould wrote the hymn "Onward Christian Soldiers." It only took him about fifteen minutes to write! As such, he fretted over whether it was completely doctrinally correct. He even told publishers that they could alter the words if they liked. But no one ever did, his words were, in fact, very good, and very well chosen. Listen to the first and third verses:

Onward Christian soldiers marching as to war with the cross of Jesus going on before! Christ, the royal master, leads against the foe, forward into battle see His banner go. Onward Christian soldiers marching as to war, with the cross of Jesus going on before!

Like a mighty army moves the church of God, brothers we are treading where the saints have trod. We are not divided all one body we, one in hope and doctrine one in charity. Onward Christian soldiers marching as to war, with the cross of Jesus going on before!

May I say that these words represent how it is actually supposed to be. But unfortunately, even from way back in the days of James, two thousand years ago, it has not always actually been that way! If we were to actually sing things the way they are in churches across the world we may find ourselves singing this:

Inward Christian soldiers marching off to war, carrying our attitudes, in through the church doors, we'll cause a disaster, and everyone will know, we have been to battle, our brothers are our foes. Inward Christian soldiers marching off to war, carrying our attitudes, in through the church doors.

Like a tiny army moves the church today, brothers we are ready, vicious things to say, we are all divided, not one body we, we have no hope no doctrine, we have no charity. Inward Christian soldiers marching off to war, carrying our attitudes, in through the church doors.

That is the type of thing that James was noticing in anger two thousand years ago as he began to write chapter four of his letter to the brethren.

The root of their problem

James 4:1 *From whence come wars and fightings among you? come they not hence, even of your lusts that war in your members?*

Two very old and well-respected commentaries have the same thing to say on this passage, and both of them are wrong. The position those old commentators took is that James was referring to the Jews who had a habit of making insurrection against the Romans and taking up swords against them. The problem with that view is that the text very clearly says "from whence come wars and fightings <u>among you</u>," not "from whence come wars and fightings <u>against Rome</u>." Whatever wars and fighting James was dealing with was happening right there in the middle of the Christians and churches that he was writing to.

This is both encouraging and discouraging, all at the same time. It is encouraging to realize that it happens everywhere. If a church realized that they were the only one that ever had trouble, that would be pretty discouraging! But it is discouraging to realize that the devil has been able to run the same play on the church of God for two thousand years and that the church has still not figured out a way to stop it!

James was writing to first century churches, churches that were being pastored by **apostles** and **disciples**, churches that had members that actually heard Jesus preach and teach, churches that had members that saw Jesus do miracles, churches that had members that saw Jesus ascend into heaven, and they still managed to have times that they fought and feuded among themselves!

You know by now that James is not a "surface" kind of guy. If there is a problem, he is going to get to the root of it or die trying. So, look at verse one again and notice that he answered the question that he asked:

James 4:1 *From whence come wars and fightings among you? come they not hence, even of your lusts that war in your members?*

James said that these wars and fightings in the midst of the church came from the lusts that warred in their members. Now let me teach you something. The vast majority of times that you see some form of the word lust in the New Testament it will be from the Greek word *epithumia*. On occasion, it will be from the word *pathos*. But twice and only twice in the New Testament will it be from the word *haydonay*. You will find those times in James 4:1 and James 4:3. Only in these two places. There is something very significant about that.

There is an English word we get from *haydonay,* it is the word hedonism. It is the idea that pleasing yourself is the highest cause of action in life. When you hear someone described as living a hedonistic lifestyle, it means that whatever they want, they find a way to get, whatever they want to do, they do, wherever they want to go, they go. They will drink, smoke, do drugs, be sexually promiscuous, steal from others, lie to get their way, they are all about pleasing self.

When James looked out at a bunch of churches that were inward Christian soldiers rather than onward Christian soldiers, he said, "I can tell you what your problem is; you are all about pleasing you."

Many years ago in the church I pastor, we had two families that ended up hating each other and drawing others into the conflict. It was not over doctrine or principle or anything like that, it was over money. Two families that called themselves Christians battled like cats and dogs over money. They called each other names; they tried to destroy each other. They have all been gone for many years. But I have kept up with them both, and do you know what? They still despise each other. Both sides wanted money, and they went to war against each other over it. That kind of thing is exactly what James meant when he said *your wars and fights are coming from the fact that you are lustful people who only want to please yourselves.*

You will often see the same thing among kids in a youth group, where two girls like the same guy, (or vice versa) and a predictable war ensues.

They are both lustful people who only want to please self.

I have seen it among men who preach who get jealous of the opportunities of others. I actually had a man many years ago storm into my office and demand to know why so and so had gotten to preach x number of times in the last several years, but he had only gotten to preach y number of times. What is that? It is lust, it is hedonism, it is the desire to please self. And by the way, a man who feels that way does not have enough God on him to deserve to preach.

I have seen it among pastors who get jealous of other pastors who get called to preach revivals when they do not.

I have seen it among parents who get jealous when someone else's child gets to sing more than their child.

Within the first year or two of the Lightning Youth Program in our church, I had a couple of families whose kids were in the program, but not really even trying, summon me to a meeting. They sat me down and said, "Preacher, we do not need to be having a situation in which some kids get trophies, and others do not."

I said, "Really? Well, tell me, do your children work hard in school?"

They said, "Yes, they do."

I said, "What kind of grades do they make?"

I could see their chests swell up with pride and their faces begin to beam and their heads begin to swell as they both told me that their children were making straight A's.

Then I said, "Do you think it is fair that the school has a situation in which some kids get A's and others only get B's or C's or D's and some even get F's? Do you think maybe the school should make sure that everybody gets A's, even the kids who are not trying anywhere near as hard as your kids are trying?"

It is amazing how quickly people can backtrack when you show them how ridiculous they are being.

This is all hedonism; it is all lust; it is all the desire to please self. And the problem is, we were not made to please self:

Revelation 4:11 *Thou art worthy, O Lord, to receive glory and honour and power: for thou hast created all things, and for thy pleasure they are and were created.*

We were made to please God! And if you could theoretically have a church full of people who wanted nothing else other than to please God, you would have a church that never had a single battle or war amongst themselves. But the fact is we are all still creatures of flesh, and as such, pleasing self comes naturally while pleasing God is something we actually have to work at.

James 4:2 *Ye lust, and have not: ye kill, and desire to have, and cannot obtain: ye fight and war, yet ye have not, because ye ask not.*

Look at the five activities that James said that they were engaging in to try and get what they wanted. He said that they lust, they kill, they desire, they fight, they war, but they still do not have what they want. I do not know if James meant that killing part literally or metaphorically, but either way the truth was still the same; they were using every fleshly means at their disposal to get what they wanted, but it was not working. They were trying to please themselves, but they were ending up unpleased. It is then that James said, "Yet ye have not, because ye ask not."

The root of their problem was lust, the solution to their problem was prayer. If they had prayed instead of fought, God would either have given them their desires or made them satisfied with what He did choose to give them. But sadly, they had already managed to mess that up as well.

The reason for their prayers

James 4:3 *Ye ask, and receive not, because ye ask amiss, that ye may consume it upon your lusts.*

James knew that when he mentioned asking, praying, that they were going to say, "But we have been praying, and it has not worked!" James beat them to the punch by telling them that he knew they had been praying, but he also knew *why* they had been praying. They were not praying to please God, they were praying to please self. They were not praying to get their hearts in tune with God's desires, they were praying to get God to give them their desires.

Albert Barnes said:

"It was not that they might have a decent and comfortable living, which would not be improper to desire, but that they might have the means of luxurious dress and living; perhaps the means of gross sensual gratifications. Prayers offered that we may have the means of sensuality and voluptuousness, we have no reason to suppose God will answer, for he has not promised to hear such prayers;"

These were people who would literally pray for God to bless them with something that His word says is wrong.

I heard a preacher tell the story of a woman in his church who had a husband who would not come to church. She asked for a meeting one day with the pastor and his wife. When they all sat down together, she said, "Pastor, I want you to know that I have met another man, and I believe he will make me a good Christian husband. So, I am leaving my husband to be with him. I've prayed about this, and this is what I am going to do."

So, you have prayed about being a worse heathen than your husband has ever thought about being. You have prayed about directly violating Scripture. You have prayed about committing adultery. Does anyone actually think that God has anything to do with those kinds of prayers? Believe me, if they do "get answered," it was not God that answered that prayer.

People are in the habit of praying prayers for the gratification of self:

Lord, let me win the lottery, I'll even tithe on it.

Lord, let me get a million-dollar Lamborghini so I can get to church faster.

Lord, let that lost girl agree to marry me so that I can win her to the Lord.

And why does God not answer prayers like that? Because it is a prayer prayed so that someone can "consume it upon his lust." It is a prayer prayed not for the glory of God, but for the sensual pleasure of man.

James was writing to people who were warring, fighting, feuding, but also praying! But their prayers were designed to do the same thing their warring and fighting and feuding were designed to do; feed their hedonistic pleasures!

The reality of their position

James 4:4 *Ye adulterers and adulteresses, know ye not that the friendship of the world is enmity with God? whosoever therefore will be a friend of the world is the enemy of God.*

Please take a moment and let the words that James used sink in.

Ye adulterers and adulteresses! Those are some very harsh words. Was everyone that James was addressing guilty of cheating on their spouse? Well, some of them likely were. But all of them were guilty of spiritual adultery, and the rest of this verse lets us know that that is what James is referring to. By them being so friendly with the world that they adopted the world's methods of getting things (wars, fightings), they were cheating on God their spouse! Ephesians 5 makes it clear that God regards the church as His bride. Doing things the world's way rather than His way is spiritual adultery for a Christian and for a church. Striving to please us rather than to please Him is spiritual adultery for a Christian and for a church.

James spoke twice here of the fact that being a friend of the world is the same as being an enemy of God. What did he mean? Did he mean that we are to be unfriendly to people who are lost? No. Jesus was referred to twice in the New Testament as the friend of sinners. Does that mean that He became such bosom buddies with them that He had a few brews with them, cursed with them, told dirty jokes with them, just became one of the guys? That is what the modern "one name seeker friendly" church is often going to tell you. But the Bible says:

Hebrews 7:26 *For such an high priest became us, who is holy, harmless, undefiled, separate from sinners, and made higher than the heavens;*

118

While being *a friend to* sinners, Jesus was still *separate from* sinners. He went to where they were, but it was to win them, not to wine and dine them. He went to where they were, but it was to confront them not to conform to them. This tells us what we need to know about James's statement that being a friend of the world is the same as being the enemy of God and the same as spiritual adultery. If being "a friend to sinners" means that we fulfill the lustful, hedonistic pleasures of our flesh, then we have become a friend to sinners in the wrong way, and we have become the enemy of God. But if being a "friend to sinners" means that we live holy and pure and deny our flesh so that we can have a good enough testimony to win them to God, we have become a friend of sinners the right way.

Based on the lustful, warring, fighting behavior of these people to whom James was writing, had they become "friends of the world" the right way or the wrong way? The wrong way! They were not trying to get the world saved so that the world could be more like Christ; they were trying to emulate the world's ways so that they could get what they wanted. And in this case the result was that they fought and feuded among themselves, they became inward Christian soldiers rather than onward Christian soldiers.

The resisting of the proud

James 4:5 *Do ye think that the scripture saith in vain, The spirit that dwelleth in us lusteth to envy?*

This verse is rather unique. James is quoting Scripture, but not any particular verse directly. There is no one verse that says this. He is thinking of all of the Old Testament verses on envy and lust in the heart of man, and he is summarizing what they say. It would be the same as if I said, "The Bible says that we ought to help our fellow church members when they have needs." There is no one verse that puts it exactly like that, but there are a host of verses that mean the exact same thing.

James was pointing out that we have inside of us a natural tendency, a strong one, to want what others have because we think it would please us. We want someone else's job, wife, husband, car, hobby, pulpit, boat, whatever. This is not something we have to be taught; it is inside of us from the cradle to the grave. We have to actually make an effort against this inward tendency to get anywhere. And it is going to require some outside help for us to have a chance to win. James knew that:

James 4:6 *But he giveth more grace. Wherefore he saith, God resisteth the proud, but giveth grace unto the humble.*

James has dropped the hammer on a problem. These folks were fighting and warring and feuding because they had, from conception, a natural desire to please their flesh, and they were giving in to that natural desire. But the hope, the light at the end of the tunnel was that God giveth "more grace." More than what? More grace than the amount of wicked spirit you have inside you lusting to envy! The word "more" is *meizon*, and it means "a greater, larger amount." The help we have available is more than enough to win this inner battle that is causing our outer battles.

Let me say that again: the help we have available is more than enough to win this inner battle that is causing our outer battles. But if that is true, why were the people to whom James was writing not winning? Look at the last half of the verse:

...Wherefore he saith, God resisteth the proud, but giveth grace unto the humble.

That "more grace" is available to the humble but not to the proud. In fact, it is even worse than that. Not only is that "more grace" not available to the proud, but God will actually resist the proud! In the context of our passage, what does that mean?

When a person is humble enough to say, "God, I have been so wrong fulfilling the desires of my flesh. And doing so has caused me to battle it out with my brothers and sisters in Christ. God, I need help, bad. I am so wicked, I need you to change me so that I can please You rather than myself," God will hear that prayer, and *He will give grace greater than the inner desires to please our flesh!*

But when a person is proud, glorying in getting his or her way, God will not only not give grace, He will resist them. Think of Pharaoh, for example. God sent Moses to tell Pharaoh to let the people go. Pharaoh got proud and said, "Who is the LORD that I should obey His voice?" And the next thing you see is God hardening Pharaoh's heart. Pharaoh at first *wouldn't* get right, so God took him a step farther and made it to where he *couldn't* get right. That is an example of God resisting the proud.

James 4:7 *Submit yourselves therefore to God. Resist the devil, and he will flee from you.*

Do you notice the similar wording between verse six and verse seven? That is by design. It is God's way of pointing out that this is an either/or proposition. We will either submit ourselves to God or to the devil. If we submit ourselves to the devil by getting proud against God, God will fight against us. But if we submit ourselves to God by resisting the devil, the devil himself will actually run from us!

Once again think of this in context. It is the devil's desire that we please him by pleasing our flesh. Doing so causes fights and feuds and wars even among brethren. This makes the devil very happy.

It is God's desire that we please Him by denying our flesh. This results in us thinking of God and others before ourselves. It results in us having more of a desire to be a blessing to other members, the pastor, the Sunday school teachers, the song leader, than to ourselves. This makes God very happy because His people stop being inward Christian soldiers and once again become onward Christian soldiers.

Some years ago, a pastor was deeply wounded by a family in his church. That family stormed out and said so many hurtful things on the way out that the church and the pastor were devastated. They kept on going, trying to work for the Lord but never could seem to recover.

As for the family, things were just as bad for them. They went through one trauma after another, and their lives were just spiraling out of control.

Then one day the pastor heard that a member of the family had a specific need, a life or death kind of thing. That pastor opened his checkbook, wrote out a generous check for them, and sent it to them along with a loving note telling them that he was praying for them and that he hoped his monetary gift would be a help to them.

And it was. That individual got the help that was needed, and everything came out just fine.

But that is not the end of the story. Everybody involved was reconciled through that act, and God Himself seemed to open the windows of heaven and start pouring blessings out all over the place. When people started thinking more of pleasing God than pleasing themselves, God responded with grace and blessings just coming down in showers.

Inward Christian soldiers break things and halt the work of the Lord. Onward Christian soldiers build things and help the work of the Lord.

Chapter Twelve
What Are You Laughing At?

James 4:8 *Draw nigh to God, and he will draw nigh to you. Cleanse your hands, ye sinners; and purify your hearts, ye double minded.* **9** *Be afflicted, and mourn, and weep: let your laughter be turned to mourning, and your joy to heaviness.* **10** *Humble yourselves in the sight of the Lord, and he shall lift you up.* **11** *Speak not evil one of another, brethren. He that speaketh evil of his brother, and judgeth his brother, speaketh evil of the law, and judgeth the law: but if thou judge the law, thou art not a doer of the law, but a judge.* **12** *There is one lawgiver, who is able to save and to destroy: who art thou that judgest another?*

In the first seven verses of this chapter, James dealt harshly with Christians battling it out with other Christians. He is still thinking along the same lines in verses eight through twelve. But in these verses, he will say something that gives us insight into how they were reacting to what they were doing. Considering the trials they were all under, it may just surprise you. We will call this section *What Are You Laughing At?*

A double minded problem

James 4:8 *Draw nigh to God, and he will draw nigh to you. Cleanse your hands, ye sinners; and purify your hearts, ye double minded.*

Backing up into the context of the previous seven verses, remember that James was dealing with people who were battling each other, which meant that they were drawing nearer to Satan and pleasing Satan while drifting farther from God and displeasing God. This meant that the "more grace" available from God in verse six was something that they were not accessing. In fact, God Himself was resisting them. The devil was not afraid of them and was not running from them, because they were not submitting themselves to God. In that context, the way that James begins verse eight makes perfect sense.

There are three things he said to them. One, get close to God again, and God will get close to you. They had drifted, badly. They were still in church, but their hearts were far, far from God. That is very often the case!

I spoke to a pastor friend recently, and he spoke of the difficulties of getting kids to grow up and actually stay in church. He said, "The only ones that do are the ones whose parents are not just in church, they are actually IN! All the way in!" A lackadaisical walk with God is not drawing nigh to God, and will not impress our children enough to keep them in.

The second thing he said to them was *cleanse your hands, ye sinners*. Here James is calling names again! In the last section, he called them adulterers and adulteresses. Now he is calling them sinners and claiming that they have dirty hands.

Please remember that James is not speaking "off the cuff"; he is speaking "under inspiration!" The words he is using are the words that God wanted him to use. The words he is using are also very picturesque, especially the part about hands in need of washing. Do you remember what Pilate did during the trial of Jesus?

Matthew 27:24 *When Pilate saw that he could prevail nothing, but that rather a tumult was made, he took water, and washed his hands before the multitude, saying, I am innocent of the blood of this just person: see ye to it.*

When a person had done something wrong, they were often spoken of as one who "had his hands dirty." Even heathens like Pilate knew that. Isaiah the prophet spoke of it as well:

Isaiah 1:15 *And when ye spread forth your hands, I will hide mine eyes from you: yea, when ye make many prayers, I will not hear: your hands are full of blood.* **16** *Wash you, make you* *clean; put away the evil of your doings from before mine eyes; cease to do evil;*

James was writing to people who were warring among themselves yet claiming to be innocent! James said, "No, I know what is going on, and you are not innocent. You are sinners with dirty hands in all of this."

The third thing he told them, though, is perhaps the most striking. He told them *purify your hearts, ye double minded.*

Here we find the heart and the mind linked together. What the mind thinks, the heart normally acts on. And in this case, the people who were doing the acting were people who had mind trouble that was causing heart trouble. Their problem is that they were double minded.

There are only two times in the entire Bible that we find the phrase "double minded." Do you remember where the other one is?

James 1:8 *A double minded man is unstable in all his ways.*

James is the only Biblical writer that ever used that phrase. Just like in chapter one, here it means vacillating, going back and forth, never getting settled.

That is the bane of modern Christianity. I would love to tell you that we are the best generation of Christians that has ever lived, but I cannot. What I can tell you is that we are perhaps the most double minded generation of Christians that has ever lived. Think about it. Can you really look at Christians today and describe them as steady, dependable, faithful, single minded, focused, solid? No, no, no.

In general, today's Christians are not even steady on the simple basics of the Christian life. Most Christians are not faithful in their church attendance, not faithful to read their Bible and pray at home during the week, not faithful in giving to the work of the Lord through their local church, not faithful in soul winning, and not faithful in living right.

There are far more Christians today that are double minded than that are single minded.

The Christians of James's day were apparently a lot like the Christians of our day. And one of the things they vacillated on was their treatment one of another. This was a double minded problem for them. Sometimes they would love each other and treat each other well, and then like a rattlesnake, they could flip completely around and bite with deadly venom. A man like James expected consistency, especially consistency in treating each other right. And the reason he expected it is because he knew that God expected it.

A doubly surprising reaction

James 4:9 *Be afflicted, and mourn, and weep: let your laughter be turned to mourning, and your joy to heaviness.* **10** *Humble yourselves in the sight of the Lord, and he shall lift you up.*

Based on these two verses, especially verse nine, how were these people responding to what they were doing, all of the fighting and feuding? They were laughing about it and having a grand time like it was all a big game! This really is doubly surprising.

It is surprising first of all in light of the very first thing that James said to them in this letter:

James 1:1 *James, a servant of God and of the Lord Jesus Christ, to the twelve tribes which are scattered abroad, greeting.* **2** *My brethren, count it all joy when ye fall into divers temptations;* **3** *Knowing this, that the trying of your faith worketh patience.*

These were people that had been driven out of their homes and lands, scattered across the world, persecuted for their faith. You would think that people like that would be very tender toward others, knowing how bad it feels to be hurt. But the bullied had become bullies themselves.

It is surprising also when you consider the fact that they were fighting their own not their enemies. Others had hurt them, and then they turned around and hurt those of their own number and laughed about it! They really did treat this like it was a game.

I wish that was just a first-century problem, but it is not. I am telling you that there are people who actually try to do damage to churches and pastors and Christians. It is a game to them. I know people who actually make a joke of how often they run the preacher off. I know people who laugh and giggle over telling lies about good people. I can think of a woman in my county who has damaged four different churches, and she thinks it is a game.

James had something to say about that. He said, *Be afflicted, and mourn, and weep: let your laughter be turned to mourning, and your joy to heaviness.* He was telling them to do this to themselves. He was demanding that they stop beating up others and start beating on themselves for what they were doing. We often speak of so and so "being too hard on himself," but the truth is that for every one person that is being too hard on himself there are probably ten that are not being nearly hard enough on themselves. Humans are much more likely to give themselves a pass on wrongdoing than they are to give themselves a spanking for wrongdoing.

But here is the thing: if we don't, HE will. Look at the next verse:

James 4:10 *Humble yourselves in the sight of the Lord, and he shall lift you up.*

Who was watching what they were doing? God was. What is the implication? You can judge yourself, or God will do it for you. If you do it yourself, God will lift you up. But what then is the implication if we do not? If we do not, God will break us down. God will absolutely deal with those who harm His children, even if it is other of His children that He has to deal with!

A doubly frightening position

James 4:11 *Speak not evil one of another, brethren. He that speaketh evil of his brother, and judgeth his brother, speaketh evil of the law, and judgeth the law: but if thou judge the law, thou art not a doer of the law, but a judge.*

It would do well at this point for us to slow down and really examine this phrase "speak not evil one of another, brethren."

Please notice that James follows up the word brethren by the use of the word brother twice. So immediately we can say one thing very conclusively. James is not dealing with what is said about not-believers and non-church members, he is dealing with what is said about believers and church members, those who give testimony to being saved. We can argue another day and from other passages about whether it is right or wrong to speak evil of politicians or murderers or the cults, but this particular passage is dealing with the saved speaking evil of the saved.

So, what does that mean? We better answer that question because, believe me, people will take the liberty to interpret it in a variety of different ways. Some, for instance, will interpret it to mean that we are never allowed to utter a negative opinion of anyone, even if it is true. But may I show you a problem with that view?

Matthew 16:23 *But he turned, and said unto Peter, Get thee behind me, Satan: thou art an offence unto me: for thou savourest not the things that be of God, but those that be of men.*

This was Jesus Himself having something extremely negative, yet true, to say about Peter who was clearly a "brother." And the list only gets longer from there:

Galatians 2:11 *But when Peter was come to Antioch, I withstood him to the face, because he was to be blamed.* **12** *For before that certain came from James, he did eat with the Gentiles: but when they were come, he withdrew and separated himself, fearing them which were of the circumcision.* **13** *And the other Jews dissembled likewise with him; insomuch that Barnabas also was carried away with their dissimulation.* **14** *But when I saw that they walked not uprightly according to the truth of the gospel, I said unto Peter before them all, If thou, being a Jew, livest after the manner of Gentiles, and not as do the Jews, why compellest thou the Gentiles to live as do the Jews?*

Here was Paul also having something very negative to say about Peter.

But may I point out something that is so extremely obvious that you probably missed it? What did James just call the Christians to whom he was writing? Adulterers, adulteresses, sinners, double minded, and dirty handed. That list seems very negative! So, if we are to conclude that these verses mean that we are never to have anything negative to say about any brethren

128

even if it is true, then we must also conclude that God was having James disobey that command while He was having him write that command!

There are times when we must, in fact, have negative things to say. If I ever cheat on my wife, it is up to my church to stand up and say, "You are disqualified; you committed adultery; you are fired." If I leave here and try to go somewhere else that does not know, it is up to my church to call them and say, "Here is what he did." If any of our members start gossiping and lying and causing division, it is up to us to obey **Romans 16:17** which says, *Now I beseech you, brethren, mark them which cause divisions and offences contrary to the doctrine which ye have learned; and avoid them.* There are many other things that can be done which actually necessitate the brethren speaking up about the brethren.

And so, it is safe to say that we have learned two things thus far. One, James is dealing with what brethren, church folks, Christians, say about other brethren/church folk/Christians. Two, He is not uttering a blanket command against us ever saying anything negative even if it is true.

So then what is he saying? When he used the word evil, he let us know. Any *word* that is in any *way* evil, we are not to speak of one another. What then are the ways a word can be evil? Here is a list that occurs to me rather quickly:

A word is evil if it is not one hundred percent true.

A word is evil if it is spoken with the wrong motive.

A word is evil if it is spoken in the wrong way.

A word is evil if it is spoken to one to whom it should not have been spoken.

I would suspect that James was dealing with all of these things. Concerning the first, people then, like now, doubtless, did not mind lying to get their way. You might want to be very careful what you believe about people based on what others tell you, because others may be lying!

We often hear, "If there's smoke there's fire!" But may I give you another possibility? Where there is smoke, there may also be an arsonist!

Are some police officers racists? Absolutely. You can find racists in every walk of life, and they ought to be dealt with. But do people often lie and claim that officers are racists?

On April 13, 2018, in Timmonsville, South Carolina, the president of a local NAACP chapter, the "Reverend" Jerrod Moultrie was stopped by a police officer for failing to use a turn signal and a problem with his license plate. He then went on social media and claimed that the officer had racially profiled him and made all kinds of racist and harassing statements. Naturally, the post went viral very quickly, and people started railing on the police.

One problem. The man was lying. All of it was caught on the officer's body cam. Another member of the good "reverend's" organization went to the police and viewed the body cam footage for himself and said that he got sick to his stomach realizing that a man he trusted had blatantly lied about something so important..." (WPDE.com)

Like I said, sometimes where there is smoke, there is fire, but sometimes where there is smoke, there is an arsonist.

Let us look at another police example. In 2015, once again in South Carolina, there was an incident. This time, a police officer shot an African America man in the back while he was running away. He claimed that he feared for his life. But then the body cam footage showed him shooting the man in the back while he was trying to run away. He lied. He point-blank lied. In *addition* to murdering somebody, he lied. (CNN.com)

James was dealing with the same kind of thing happening in churches. Christians were literally lying about each other and destroying each other's lives. You need to be aware that that does happen from time to time. And please remember what I said, a word is evil if it is not one hundred percent true. Why do I say that? Because people normally are crafty enough to take ninety-nine percent truth and add one percent of a lie to it. That one percent of a lie makes it just as wrong and just as deadly as a one hundred percent lie, but it also makes it much harder to detect.

If I say, "Brother-so-and-so was in Paris last week, and while he was there, he stole a valuable painting from the

Louvre." What have I accused him of? Stealing. How much of what I said was a lie? All of it, one hundred percent. He was not in Paris, he was not in the Louvre, and he did not take a painting.

But what if I say, "Brother-so-and-so, the mechanic, was in his motor building shop last week, a customer came in, and brother so and so shafted the guy. Charged him $2000 for an engine job that should have only cost $1000." What have I accused him of? Stealing. How much of what I said was a lie? Only a little bitty part of it! He was in his shop, he did do an engine job, he did charge the guy, but he did not shaft him. He actually gave him a very fair price.

But which of my two lies are you more likely to believe? The second one, because so much of what I said in the second one is true! But either way, I have accused him of stealing; either way, I have lied!

You do realize that people do this kind of thing, don't you? People are very good about taking ninety-nine percent truth and mixing in one percent lie and destroying a reputation by that mixture. It is doubtless one thing that James had in mind when he warned them against speaking evil.

Now to the second item on the list. A word is also evil if it is spoken with the wrong motive. In other words, why are you saying what you say?

We tried very hard when our children were young to help them to understand this principle. We did not want them tattling just to try to get each other in trouble. So, we told them that if any of them were doing something that was going to cause harm of any kind to themselves or others and that they found out about it, they needed to come to tell us. But if they were coming to tell us something just because they wanted to get the other one in trouble, that was just tattling, and we really did not want to hear it.

Even in a church setting, sometimes you will find people coming in and speaking to the pastor because they are concerned for people and do not want to see them hurt themselves or others with what they are doing, but sometimes you will find people coming in speaking to the pastor with sadistic glee because they have managed to catch someone doing something wrong, and they just want to see the hammer fall.

A pastor friend of mine had a middle-aged couple in his church come to him in an extreme state of "righteous indignation." They had just learned that a teenage girl in the church had gotten pregnant out of wedlock, and they demanded that she be dragged in front of the church and dealt with in the harshest possible manner.

As it turns out, the pastor was already aware of the situation. In fact, he was aware of a particular part of the situation that the couple standing in front of him was not aware of, namely, the fact that the daddy of the baby that the girl was carrying was their son!

It was amazing, really, how their tune changed when he brought that fact to their attention. Suddenly they began to feel very merciful over the whole situation and conveyed their expectations that the pastor would be merciful as well.

So, what do you think their motive was in coming to the pastor with that information? They just wanted someone to be punished until they found out that their own son was involved.

Third item. A word is evil if it is spoken to one to whom it should not have been spoken.

Years ago, when I was in one of the Bible colleges from which I earned a degree, the issue of Calvinism came up. Many of the upperclassmen began to embrace that dangerous and unbiblical doctrine. But worse still, they begin to talk to all of the underclassmen about it, young and impressionable freshmen and sophomores.

When this came to the attention of the staff and faculty, a student assembly was held. The upperclassmen were called down for what they were doing; it was an incredibly tense time. One of the ringleaders stood up and very piously said, "Are we in an educational institution where it is unsafe to even ask questions about something like this?"

That question seemed to throw the staff member holding the meeting a little bit off guard. But for whatever reason, God immediately gave me the right words. I stood up at once and said, "The problem is not the fact that you were asking questions about something like this; the problem is the fact that you are asking young students about it as opposed to old professors about it. The professors are able to handle it; the students aren't, and you know it."

What you say can either be right or wrong depending on who you say it to. People on Facebook have no business viewing your dirty laundry or hearing about your grievances with your church or anyone in your church.

Now go back to verse eleven again. James said *He that speaketh evil of his brother, and judgeth his brother, speaketh evil of the law, and judgeth the law:*

Judges the law... what does that mean? Adam Clarke said:

> The law condemns all evil speaking and detraction. He who is guilty of these, and allows himself in these vices, in effect judges and condemns the law; i.e., he considers it unworthy to be kept, and that it is no sin to break it. (6:821)

That is jaw-droppingly pointed. If you and I speak evil of each other, we are literally looking at God and saying, "Your commandments on this subject aren't important enough for me to keep." Can you imagine such spiritual arrogance!

By the multiple uses of the word "judge" in verse eleven, we learn something about what evil things they were saying. They were becoming Pharisee-like.

Years ago, we had a lady in our church, and I use the word "lady" lightly, with a tongue so long that if she laid it on the altar it would lap over on both ends and roll out the side door into the parking lot. There is a gentleman in our church who loves to praise the Lord, and I enjoy hearing it. This woman went to the man's wife and said, "You know, don't you, that he is just doing all of that shouting and praising for show; he isn't for real."

That is amazing. What is even more amazing is that the wife had enough composure not to put her fist completely down her face right there in front of God and everybody.

But this is how Christians often get. They can see nothing but bad in everyone but themselves, and they are more than willing to open their mouths and talk about it.

James 4:12 *There is one lawgiver, who is able to save and to destroy: who art thou that judgest another?*

Who is this one lawgiver? That would be Jesus. We have no right to take His place. We have no right to demand that He get off the throne so we can sit in His place and set people straight. But many do.

And when that happens, believe me, our Lord does not bow to their demands, acquiesce, and allow them to take His spot on the throne of judgment; He actually turns His judgment toward them, not the people that they are pointing at.

James had a question. It basically went like this, "What are you laughing at? What do you find so funny about ripping each other to shreds with your mouths?"

God did not find it funny, and neither should we, ever.

The tongue. Why did God give us that thing? May I give you just one answer from Scripture?

Proverbs 18:21 *Death and life are in the power of the tongue: and they that love it shall eat the fruit thereof.*

The tongue that can bring death can also bring life. The same tongue that Christians often use to rip each other to shreds can be used to build each other up and help each other to go on for Christ one more day and another day and another day and another day. You have no idea the impact you can have on others with just a kind word or two.

True story. Mary had grown up knowing that she was different from the other kids, and she hated it. She was born with a cleft palate and had to bear the jokes and stares of cruel children who teased her non-stop about her misshaped lip, crooked nose, and garbled speech. With all the teasing, Mary grew up hating the fact that she was "different." She was convinced that no one, outside her family, could ever love her ... until she entered Mrs. Leonard's class.

Mrs. Leonard had a warm smile, a round face, and shiny brown hair. While everyone in her class liked her, Mary came to love Mrs. Leonard. In the 1950s, it was common for teachers to give their children an annual hearing test. However, in Mary's case, in addition to her cleft palate, she was barely able to hear out of one ear. Determined not to let the other children have another "difference" to point out, she would cheat on the test each year. The "whisper test" was given by having a child walk to the classroom door, turn sideways, close one ear with a finger, and then repeat something which the teacher whispered. Mary turned her bad ear towards her teacher and pretended to cover her good ear, but actually didn't, since she could hear very well out of that one. She knew that teachers would often say things like, "The sky is blue," or "What color are your shoes?" But not on that day. Surely, God put seven words in Mrs. Leonard's mouth that changed Mary's life forever. When the "Whisper test" came, out of her one good ear Mary heard the words: "I wish you were my little girl."

Her life was never the same. (bible.org)

If you are hurting people with your words, especially other Christians, I have a question for you; "What are you laughing at?" You have nothing to laugh at. You do not even have anything to smile about. In order for you to have something to smile about, you need to start building people up with your words, not tearing them down.

Chapter Thirteen
Little Orphan Annie Theology

James 4:13 *Go to now, ye that say, To day or to morrow we will go into such a city, and continue there a year, and buy and sell, and get gain:* **14** *Whereas ye know not what shall be on the morrow. For what is your life? It is even a vapour, that appeareth for a little time, and then vanisheth away.* **15** *For that ye ought to say, If the Lord will, we shall live, and do this, or that.* **16** *But now ye rejoice in your boastings: all such rejoicing is evil.* **17** *Therefore to him that knoweth to do good, and doeth it not, to him it is sin.*

There are times in the book of James when it is very interesting to try and follow his thoughts from one place to the next. In these seven verses, it is evident that he has changed subjects, but I think we can see how he got from one to the next. He has spent twelve verses rebuking them for the way that they were feuding and fighting and judging one another. They had gotten so presumptuous that they were becoming "judges over the law!" They were aware that God's law and man's law forbad the things they were doing, but they decided to do them anyway. It seems to be that very presumption that led to their next error and James's next rebuke. We will call this section *Little Orphan Annie Theology*.

Many years ago, a certain curly red-headed little girl had a song to sing:

The sun'll come out tomorrow, bet your bottom dollar that tomorrow there'll be sun! Just thinkin' about tomorrow clears away the cobwebs, and the sorrow 'Til there's none!

When I'm stuck with a day, that's gray and lonely, I just stick out my chin, and grin, and say, Oh

The sun'll come out tomorrow so ya gotta hang on 'til tomorrow

Come what may...

Tomorrow! Tomorrow! I love ya Tomorrow! You're always

A day away!

Now, with all due respect to a kid who managed to ingratiate herself to Daddy Warbucks, I have some questions. One: how exactly do you know that the sun will, in fact, come out tomorrow? It seems to me that professional weather forecasters with eight years of college and seven-figure salaries get the weather forecast for the next day right around six percent of the time. Do you really want to "bet your bottom dollar" on something that iffy? Should you not maybe invest that bottom dollar and try to pay off debts and build up a savings account?

You say, "Preacher, you are being just a bit ridiculous; it is just a happy song." Yes, yes, I know that. But there is a point, here, and an important one. So, imagine yourself watching James listening to Little Orphan Annie sing, and let's get into the text and see what he has to say.

The pride of presumption

James 4:13 *Go to now, ye that say, To day or to morrow we will go into such a city, and continue there a year, and buy and sell, and get gain:*

In the Bible, you will find that the words "go to" are used quite differently than the way that we use them today. When we say "go to," there will be a location at the end of it. Sometimes when someone tells you to "go to," the location that follows is not a particularly pleasant one! When the words "go to" are used in the Bible, they are often used in a completely different way.

138

In fact, the first three times they are used in the Bible they are used in this odd way:

Genesis 11:3 *And they said one to another, Go to, let us make brick, and burn them throughly. And they had brick for stone, and slime had they for morter.*

Genesis 11:4 *And they said, Go to, let us build us a city and a tower, whose top may reach unto heaven; and let us make us a name, lest we be scattered abroad upon the face of the whole earth.*

Genesis 11:7 *Go to, let us go down, and there confound their language, that they may not understand one another's speech.*

The men at the tower of Babel used "go to" the same way that James did in our text. In our modern language, we would say "come on!" It is not anything to do with location. There is a sports show called "Come On, Man!" That is actually very much like what James is saying as we begin this section. Look at it again:

James 4:13 *Go to now, ye that say, To day or to morrow we will go into such a city, and continue there a year, and buy and sell, and get gain:*

"Come on, you people that are saying this..." Do you see how that lets us into the mind of James on this subject? He was acting as if he could not believe what he was hearing. So, what was he hearing?

The persecuted Christians to whom James was writing had a really good plan for present-day prosperity. And as far as the plan itself, there was not actually anything wrong with it. They planned to *"go into such a city, and continue there a year, and buy and sell, and get gain."*

Now let me state right up front that there are some positives with this plan. The main positive that I see is that it involved business instead of waiting for a handout. It involved, are you ready, *capitalism.* It involved actually doing things the way God intended, working and investing and growing your wealth by honest means.

The problem was not with the plan; the problem was with the presumption behind it. There are four "we wills" either stated or implied. We **will** go into that city, we **will** stay there a year, we **will** buy and sell, we **will** make a profit.

They were demonstrating the pride of presumption. In other words, they very much viewed all of these four "we wills" as being entirely up to them. This was all about their intelligence and their ability and their skill. There was no thought in their mind that perhaps they would not be able to do any of this or perhaps circumstances beyond their control may arise. There was no humility in their plans because they viewed themselves as omnipotent in the carrying out of those plans.

The problem of presumption

James 4:14 *Whereas ye know not what shall be on the morrow. For what is your life? It is even a vapour, that appeareth for a little time, and then vanisheth away.*

It did not take James long to state the obvious problem: *ye know not what shall be on the morrow.*

Tell me something, please; what is going to happen tomorrow?

When you get completely, totally factual, the only legitimate answer is, "I have no idea."

Have you ever at the end of one day laid out your plans for the next day only to have the next day dawn and your entire world end up in such a disjointed mess that the entire day went completely different from all of your plans?

The complexion of life, as James states it, furthers this idea. Life is just a vapor that appears for a small time and then vanishes away. He is talking about the breath that you would blow into the cold air in the winter. It is there for a moment and then it is gone.

As a pastor, I have been at many deathbeds. Do you know what I have never heard a single time? Not once have I ever heard a person in the last few hours of life say, "Wow, I never dreamed it would take this long for me to get through life! It seems like I have been alive forever!"

Nope. It is always like a person blowing a vapor and then gone. And even within the realm of that short life, every single day proves to us again and again that we will have to expect the unexpected.

Because of how uncertain life is, there is a great big difference between planning and presuming. Presuming leaves out the possibility that God may have other plans. Planning recognizes that the final result really is not up to you. You plan, you work, but since only God knows everything that will be happening around you and your plans, the final result is up to Him.

I plan on living a very long time. Disease or accident may have other ideas.

A plan for dealing with presumption

James 4:15 *For that ye ought to say, If the Lord will, we shall live, and do this, or that.*

Presumption is the problem; but there is a way to deal with it, as this verse demonstrates. The way to deal with presumption is to constantly remember and verbalize the "missing element" that causes it: the will of God! If the Lord "does not will," our plans mean nothing!

When James said, *ye ought to say,* he literally meant that. We ought to say it. We ought to say, "If the Lord wills," or "Lord willing" when speaking of our future plans.

Now, here is where the smug, overly pious, Pharisaical brethren will stick out their long pointy noses and have a few words to say: "This is much more than just words! It is an attitude of the heart! Without that proper heart attitude, the words mean nothing."

Well, maybe you are right, but here is the thing; James, in the Bible, actually said, *ye ought to say.* Did James not know that the important thing is the attitude of the heart? Certainly. But he also knew what pointy nosed brethren do not seem to know; our words impact our heart.

When you start thanking God out loud, even when you do not feel like it, what happens to your heart? It becomes more thankful.

When you start speaking loving words to your spouse even when you do not feel like it, what happens to your heart? It begins to feel more loving.

When we make it a habit of saying, "Lord willing," what is our heart constantly being reminded of? The fact that we are dependent upon God's will!

And notice how widely James applied this truth:

James 4:15 *For that ye ought to say, If the Lord will, we shall live, and do **this**, or **that**.*

Are those words "this" and "that" very specific or very general? They are very general. "This" or "that" may be used to refer to running a business or selling a car or brushing your teeth or going to bed or eating a meal or blowing your nose or running for president.

James was trying to point out that the way to deal with presumption is to recognize that in every area of our lives, great or small, God is still sovereign.

Let me show you a man who very clearly forgot that:

Luke 12:16 *And he spake a parable unto them, saying, The ground of a certain rich man brought forth plentifully:* **17** *And he thought within himself, saying, What shall I do, because I have no room where to bestow my fruits?* **18** *And he said, This will I do: I will pull down my barns, and build greater; and there will I bestow all my fruits and my goods.* **19** *And I will say to my soul, Soul, thou hast much goods laid up for many years; take thine ease, eat, drink, and be merry.* **20** *But God said unto him, Thou fool, this night thy soul shall be required of thee: then whose shall those things be, which thou hast provided?*

Does this man not sound exactly like what James was describing? I WILL pull down my barns, I WILL build greater, I WILL put all my good in those barns, I WILL eat drink and be merry for many years.

Not one time did he ever say, "If the Lord will," everything was "I will."

And God called him a fool. And God still calls people fools who behave that way. If you are going through life saying, "I will go to college, and I will get a degree, and I will start a career, and I will buy a car and I will have a family, and I will become successful and I will, I will, I will," then the God of heaven is shaking His head at you and saying, "You fool..."

The plan for dealing with presumption is to constantly verbalize that God's will is the deciding factor in everything.

The putrification of presumption

James 4:16 *But now ye rejoice in your boastings: all such rejoicing is evil.*

This verse is so funny that it is almost sad. They were not just bragging about what they were going to do; they were also rejoicing over the fact that they were bragging!

James said, "That is evil!"

This was the height of "self-sufficiency" apart from God. One evil was being joined by another. Presumption is like that; it makes everything else rotten.

I have never seen a presumptuous person who was not also eaten up with other sins on top of that sin. A person who fancies himself or herself "a self-made man" or a "self-made woman" may be right, if what they intended to make was a clown.

And preachers can be some of the world's worst at this. I was at a meeting a few years ago, and the moderator in charge of the meeting had two instructions. One, take half an hour. Two, glorify the Lord. A very pompous preacher stood up, preached for an hour and a half, mentioned himself roughly a thousand times, and I literally do not remember him ever actually mentioning the Lord.

The personal responsibility against presumption

James 4:17 *Therefore to him that knoweth to do good, and doeth it not, to him it is sin.*

This is one of those general truths in Scripture that also has a specific context. In all things, if you know that you are supposed to do something good and yet you do not do it, you have sinned.

Church attendance, tithing, witnessing, praying, Bible reading, serving.

But though that is a general truth, have you ever stopped to consider the very specific context James placed it in?

They knew they should have acknowledged God and deferred to His will (v.15) but did not (v.16) and therefore had sinned. They had Little Orphan Annie theology; they believed that their plans and their efforts were enough. And so they ignored the "good thing" of verbalizing their dependence on God's will and actually meaning it.

Chapter Fourteen
Turning the Barrel Outward

James 5:1 *Go to now, ye rich men, weep and howl for your miseries that shall come upon you.* **2** *Your riches are corrupted, and your garments are motheaten.* **3** *Your gold and silver is cankered; and the rust of them shall be a witness against you, and shall eat your flesh as it were fire. Ye have heaped treasure together for the last days.* **4** *Behold, the hire of the labourers who have reaped down your fields, which is of you kept back by fraud, crieth: and the cries of them which have reaped are entered into the ears of the Lord of sabaoth.* **5** *Ye have lived in pleasure on the earth, and been wanton; ye have nourished your hearts, as in a day of slaughter.* **6** *Ye have condemned and killed the just; and he doth not resist you.* **7** *Be patient therefore, brethren, unto the coming of the Lord. Behold, the husbandman waiteth for the precious fruit of the earth, and hath long patience for it, until he receive the early and latter rain.* **8** *Be ye also patient; stablish your hearts: for the coming of the Lord draweth nigh.*

For four chapters, James has had the barrel of the gun turned inward, dealing with the church. Now he will deal with those who are hurting those in the church.

Here is one way we know this for sure:

James 5:6 *Ye have condemned and killed the just; and he doth not resist you.*

In James's day, there were people of wealth and means who, rather than using those material blessings for good, were using them as weapons against God's people. Men like George Soros in our day, the multi-billionaire who despises God and righteousness and throws his wealth behind every liberal cause he can find:

He is the one that "helped kick-start America's medical marijuana movement. In the early 2000s, he became a vocal backer of same-sex marriage efforts." (opensociety foundations.org)

Listen to this passage from the L.A. Times in 2004:

"His motto, 'If I spend enough, I will make it right,' is the essence of his articulated ideas about changing society.

"It seems that Soros believes he was anointed by God. 'I fancied myself as some kind of god ...' he once wrote. 'If truth be known, I carried some rather potent messianic fantasies with me from childhood, which I felt I had to control, otherwise they might get me in trouble.'

"When asked by Britain's Independent newspaper to elaborate on that passage, Soros said, 'It is a sort of disease when you consider yourself some kind of god, the creator of everything, but I feel comfortable about it now since I began to live it out.'

"Despite his reputation as an international philanthropist, Soros remains candid about his true charitable tendencies. 'I am sort of a deus ex machina,' Soros told the New York Times in 1994. 'I am something unnatural. I'm very comfortable with my public persona because it is one I have created for myself." (Latimes.com)

Listen to me carefully. Soros is wicked and wealthy. But wealth is never the problem; being rich is not a sin. Some of Christ's own most devoted followers were quite wealthy:

Matthew 27:57 *When the even was come, there came a rich man of Arimathaea, named Joseph, who also himself was*

Jesus' disciple: **58** *He went to Pilate, and begged the body of Jesus. Then Pilate commanded the body to be delivered.* **59** *And when Joseph had taken the body, he wrapped it in a clean linen cloth,* **60** *And laid it in his own new tomb, which he had hewn out in the rock: and he rolled a great stone to the door of the sepulchre, and departed.*

Joseph used his wealth for good. He is not the kind of rich person James had in mind in our text. James had another type of rich person altogether in mind.

A surprising turn

James 5:1 *Go to now, ye rich men, weep and howl for your miseries that shall come upon you.*

James, in our day, would have been considered an oddity: a preacher who dared to have harsh things to say to wicked rich people, whether outside of or even a member of a church. That, especially in our day where the "prosperity gospel" is so prevalent, is almost unheard of!

The church had to be surprised to hear this turn, and after the scalding they had been getting they were probably pretty glad that James had turned his attention to others.

Let me tell you, though, who else was likely very surprised; whatever rich people who had been guilty of what James was describing were probably stunned that he would dare to confront them in this manner.

James told them to *weep and howl for your miseries that shall come upon you.* That is some very picturesque writing. Not just cry, but *weep and howl for your miseries that shall come upon you.*

Whatever these wicked, wealthy people were doing, and we will find more about that as we get into the chapter, James was looking ahead at what was absolutely certainly coming to them and warning them that they were going to regret their behavior in the most profound way possible.

I know this may sound surprising, but wealth is no protection against the judging hand of God. People like George Soros can rest in the power of their billions, and a merciful God will give them time, often lots of time to repent.

But not forever. No one gets forever. Every wicked man or woman will have a day of judgment either in this life or the next or both.

A shocking prophecy

James 5:2 *Your riches are corrupted, and your garments are motheaten.* **3** *Your gold and silver is cankered* **(rusted over)***; and the rust of them shall be a witness against you, and shall eat your flesh as it were fire. Ye have heaped treasure together for the last days.*

When James spoke here, he was speaking of a future event as a present reality, just like the prophets of old.

Commentator Adam Clarke paraphrased these words this way:

> "Your putrefied stores, your moth-eaten garments, and your tarnished coin, are so many proofs that it was not for want of property that you assisted not the poor, but through a principle of avarice; loving money, not for the sake of what it could procure, but for its own sake, which is the genuine principle of the miser.

> "Shall eat your flesh as it were fire. This is a very bold and sublime figure. He represents the rust of their coin as becoming a canker that should produce gangrenes and... ulcers in their flesh, till it should be eaten away from their bones.

> "Ye have heaped treasure together for the last days. The day of judgment; the closing scenes of this world. You have been heaping up treasure; but it will be treasure of a different kind from what you have supposed." (6:824)

Now please allow me to give my take on these words. James was saying in so many words, "You are utterly consumed day and night with the thought of the wealth that you have and with thoughts of making it even greater than it already is. It will never be enough for you. You have enough for a million lifetimes, yet when it comes to godliness, you are absolutely bankrupt. You are the poorest person on earth and are just too dumb to realize it. There will come a day when the very wealth that you have stored up is going to seem like the cruelest joke of all. You are going to face judgment, and all of that wealth will be worth absolutely less than nothing."

Does that sound very similar to something that Jesus Himself said?

Mark 8:34 *And when he had called the people unto him with his disciples also, he said unto them, Whosoever will come after me, let him deny himself, and take up his cross, and follow me.* **35** *For whosoever will save his life shall lose it; but whosoever shall lose his life for my sake and the gospel's, the same shall save it.* **36** *For what shall it profit a man, if he shall gain the whole world, and lose his own soul?* **37** *Or what shall a man give in exchange for his soul?*

After three seconds in hell, a person would be willing to give the wealth of a thousand worlds to get out. But there is not enough wealth, not in ten billion worlds. Why? Because salvation is free. That realization will make a person's trust in their wealth the cruelest joke of all, and the punch line will last for all eternity.

A straightforward accusation

James 5:4 *Behold, the hire of the labourers who have reaped down your fields, which is of you kept back by fraud, crieth: and the cries of them which have reaped are entered into the ears of the Lord of sabaoth.*

It is pretty reasonable to assume here in America that most everyone that is in some way employed by someone else probably receives a paycheck either at the end of the week or the end of every two weeks.

But in the agricultural world of Bible times, that was not the case:

Matthew 20:1 *For the kingdom of heaven is like unto a man that is an householder, which went out early in the morning to hire labourers into his vineyard.* **2** *And when he had agreed with the labourers for a penny a day, he sent them into his vineyard.* **3** *And he went out about the third hour, and saw others* *standing idle in the marketplace,* **4** *And said unto them; Go ye also into the vineyard, and whatsoever is right I will give you. And they went their way.* **5** *Again he went out about the sixth and ninth hour, and did likewise.* **6** *And about the eleventh hour he went out, and found others standing idle, and saith unto them, Why stand ye here all the day idle?* **7** *They say unto him, Because no man hath hired us. He saith unto them, Go ye also into the vineyard; and whatsoever is right, that shall ye receive.* **8** *So when even was come, the lord of the vineyard saith unto his steward, Call the labourers, and give them their hire, beginning from the last unto the first.* **9** *And when they came that were hired about the eleventh hour, they received every man a penny.*

These workers were paid at the end of every single day. And what you read in this account was not an oddity; it was actually commanded by the Old Testament law:

Leviticus 19:13 *Thou shalt not defraud thy neighbour, neither rob him: the wages of him that is hired shall not abide with thee all night until the morning.*

Deuteronomy 24:15 *At his day thou shalt give him his hire, neither shall the sun go down upon it; for he is poor, and setteth his heart upon it: lest he cry against thee unto the LORD, and it be sin unto thee.*

Everyone understood this. It was common practice in the ancient world. And yet there were men of wealth and means who were having people work their fields for them and, in James's words, defrauding them of their wages day by day.

This was not spoken as a probability; James stated it outright as an accusation. And remember that he was dealing with people who were hurting members of the church, members of the body of Christ. In other words, some people that he dearly loved, some brothers and sisters in Christ, were being taken advantage of by wealthy employers, and James, the man of God, was not going to sit back quietly and not have something to say about it.

Notice again what he did say about it:

James 5:4 *Behold, the hire of the labourers who have reaped down your fields, which is of you kept back by fraud,* *crieth: and the cries of them which have reaped are entered into the ears of the Lord of sabaoth.*

These Christians were working hard and honest. They had every right to expect their pay at the end of the day. They were being defrauded, though, by wealthy employers. They were then turning and crying to the God of heaven over what was happening. James said that their cries had entered into the ears of the "Lord of sabaoth."

You will definitely want to know what that word means. It looks and sounds a great deal like the word Sabbath, which spoke of a day of rest, but it is an entirely different word with a radically different meaning.

The word *sabaoth* means hosts or armies. God was being described here in a militaristic term. He is being described as a God capable of bringing great vengeance on those who have been wronged.

Our God is literally the God over the armies of heaven. Every angel and mighty creature was created by Him and is under His sole command. That is not Someone you want angry with you. But the implication is quite clear; do wrong to God's people, and God will be angry with you.

The world quite often looks at Christians as helpless victims. They believe they can take advantage of them anytime they choose to do so. And while it is true that we do not have armies at our command, is also true that the God we are crying to does have armies at His command.

Christian, on those days that you feel like you are being taken advantage of, there is a sharp promise of Scripture you may want to lean on:

Romans 12:19 *Dearly beloved, avenge not yourselves, but rather give place unto wrath: for it is written, Vengeance is mine; I will repay, saith the Lord.*

It is very, very tempting to lash back at people. Some years ago in Brazil, a group of indigenous Indians was denied access to speak to the president, because they were not wearing neckties. So they then sent word that from then on, anyone from the government who wished to enter one of their villages would only be allowed to enter if he was wearing a feather headdress and body paint... (Sermonillustrations.com, vengeance)

Taking vengeance is not necessary for a child of God, though, not even against rich oppressors. God Himself has promised to take vengeance on our behalf.

A sorry lifestyle

James 5:5 *Ye have lived in pleasure on the earth, and been wanton; ye have nourished your hearts, as in a day of slaughter.*

Adam Clarke paraphrased this verse this way:

"Ye have lived in pleasure. Ye have lived luxuriously; feeding yourselves without fear, pampering the flesh.

"And been wanton. Ye have lived lasciviously. Ye have indulged all your sinful and sensual appetites to the uttermost; and your lives have been scandalous.

"Ye have nourished your hearts. Ye have fattened your hearts, and have rendered them incapable of feeling, as in a day of slaughter, a day of sacrifice, where many victims are offered at once, and where the people feast upon the sacrifices; many, no doubt, turning, on that occasion, a holy ordinance into a riotous festival." (6:824)

And now once again let me give you my take on that. James was basically saying, "You have lived high on the hog, but every bit of it has been at the expense of others."

James 5:6 *Ye have condemned and killed the just; and he doth not resist you.*

This is a perfect description of what was happening in the first century AD. James has already alluded to this once before in this book:

James 2:6 *But ye have despised the poor. Do not rich men oppress you, and draw you before the judgment seats?*

152

Under the guise of the law, people with wealth and connections were dragging Christians into court and destroying them financially or even literally taking their lives.

If you have even remotely been paying attention to what is happening in America over these last few years, none of that comes as a surprise to you.

In June 2018 the Supreme Court gave a ruling on the Masterpiece Cake Shop case. For those who are somehow unaware of that case, a few years ago, two gay men in Colorado bypassed dozens of other bakeries and walked into the bakery owned by Jack Phillips, a very devout Christian.

They asked him to create a custom cake for their wedding. He refused to do so. He offered to sell them anything that was in his shop or to make them a cake for any other type of event that did not violate his conscience, but that is not what they were interested in. They hauled this man before the Colorado Civil Rights Commission, one of the most inappropriately named bodies in America. The Colorado Civil Rights Commission bullied Phillips and sought to punish him for his religious views, even at one point comparing his cake refusal to the Holocaust.

Wicked men with money and power did everything they could to destroy Jack Phillips. The Supreme Court of the United States acknowledged that and ruled in favor of Mr. Phillips.

But that is not an odd thing; it is an ongoing attack. A florist, a sweet grandmother named Baronnelle Stutzman is going through the exact same kind of attack right now, and her case is making its way to the Supreme Court.

In case you do not understand, let me make it very clear to you. None of these cases have anything to do with wedding cakes or flowers. In every single one of these cases, there are multiple bakers and multiple florists who would be more than willing to do what these people are looking for. But they are very specifically bypassing those other bakers and florists and, I might add, they are also very carefully avoiding any Muslim bakeries and florists, and they are actively seeking out Christians to destroy.

Using your wealth to live luxuriously at the expense of believers is absolutely a sorry lifestyle.

A strong encouragement

James 5:7 *Be patient therefore, brethren, unto the coming of the Lord. Behold, the husbandman waiteth for the precious fruit of the earth, and hath long patience for it, until he receive the early and latter rain. 8 Be ye also patient; stablish your hearts: for the coming of the Lord draweth nigh.*

James has had a lot to say thus far, all of it directed toward men of wealth and power who were trying to abuse Christians. But as we enter verses seven and eight, James is no longer dealing with those people; instead, he is turning his attention to those Christians themselves and telling them how to respond. He wants to give them some encouragement to keep them going even in the midst of all the persecution they have to endure.

And my, my, my what encouragement he gives!

James 5:7 *Be patient therefore, brethren, unto the coming of the Lord. Behold, the husbandman waiteth for the precious fruit of the earth, and hath long patience for it, until he receive the early and latter rain.*

James had already spent some time using the illustration of agriculture. Now he is doing so again. He tells these Christians who are undergoing trials at the hands of wealthy and powerful people to be patient unto the coming of the Lord. Then he says, *"Behold, the husbandman waiteth for the precious fruit of the earth, and hath long patience for it, until he receive the early and latter rain."*

There were two main periods of rain in Judea and in between those two main periods of rain a whole lot of dry times.

The first period of rain came in early November right after the seeds were sown. The second main period of rain came in April just as the crops were coming to full ripeness.

Put yourself in the position of a farmer in those days. You have sown your seeds, and a couple of weeks later the early rains have fallen letting you know that your crops are going to spring up at some point. But then months and months and months go by with little to no rain. After a while you get nervous. Then nervousness gives way to panic. Panic eventually gives way to very near hopelessness.

But then one day your little son comes running in from the field and says, "Daddy! Daddy! Guess what! The rain is falling. Daddy, the crops are going to make it!"

You run to the door, fling it wide open, and sure enough that precious April rain is falling. After months and months, you wondered if things would ever get better, and now you know that you should have trusted the Lord all along.

This is the picture that James is painting here. James is dealing with Christians who are living right, and because of that, they feel like things ought to be going better for them. And yet they are not going better. Wealthy and powerful men are still trying to destroy them, and in many cases, it seems like they are succeeding and getting by with it.

James said, "Just be patient. You had the early rain; you are in the dry time now; it looks like evil is winning and righteousness is losing, but God never fails to send that latter rain."

Years ago, we took a stand in our church on what is very clearly a biblical truth: a real church is never a "skin color" church. There is no such thing as a real church that is a white church or black church or Hispanic church. There is just the church. And the church, Christ's church, the real church, is open to anyone regardless of how much melanin is in their skin.

When we took that stand, we took a hit. Not only did we lose some people, but another church a great way off publicly ripped into us. It was bad. They openly taught that there should be a white church here and a black church there and a Hispanic church there and an oriental church over there and Native American church there and that any mixing of peoples was an abomination in the sight of God, and that we at Cornerstone, especially me, were pretty much the devil for "promoting that abomination."

But do you know what happened? We just patiently kept on doing what was right, we made it through the dry time, and God sent the latter rains. You say, "Preacher, what do you mean by that?" What I mean by that is, not only have we done fine, but that church that fought against us went through an upheaval over the wrong position they were taking in regard to what we were doing, and now not only are we still in the right, but their entire church including the pastor came around to that which was right.

Just be patient! God may not send all the rain you want just when you think you need it, but the latter rains are coming.

James 5:8 *Be ye also patient; stablish your hearts: for the coming of the Lord draweth nigh.*

One last bit of encouragement from James. We are not just waiting for the rain; we are waiting for the return. No matter what you are facing, even if you are being beaten down by some wealthy and powerful attacker, a sound is coming that is going to change everything. When the trumpet sounds, it will be like a bell being sounded inside the ring where a fight is taking place. The instant that trumpet sounds, Heaven's Referee will step in, our hands will be raised in triumph, we will be wearing the victor's belt, we will be heading for the celebration, and we will have all eternity to thank God that we had something much more precious than riches.

As I said earlier, there is nothing wrong with wealth and riches. I gave you the example of Joseph of Arimathea who was a wealthy follower of Christ. When Christians have wealth and riches, it can actually be a tremendous blessing. There is no virtue in poverty. I encourage all of our young people to have great careers where they can make a lot of money if that is the Lord's will for them. If God chooses instead to call them to the ministry, that is wonderful too. But Christian doctors and Christian lawyers and Christian business owners and Christian dentists and Christian pharmacists can be a huge blessing and a huge help by the resources that God has given them. So again, wealth and riches by themselves are not sinful.

But if that is what we are setting our hearts on, if that is our goal for life, then we really do not know God, or we are at minimum grievously backslidden and not putting Him first, and we will very likely become just like the rich men of James's day who not only did not use their wealth for good, they actively used it for evil.

What are you doing with the resources that God has given you? Young people, what do you intend to do if God allows you to become rich? I believe two of the saddest cases you will ever see in time or eternity are first, like what James is describing where someone is all about wealth and actually uses it for wicked purposes and then has to face God to answer for that, or second, someone who had great wealth and yet never used any of it to further the cause of Christ.

Whatever you have, make a real difference with it.

Recently, I preached a tent revival in Danville, Virginia. One of those tents is about $20,000; they are not cheap items. And yet a man up there has one, and this is what he does with it. He takes it around and sets it up so the people can preach the gospel. He is using his wealth and resources for that purpose.

I preached that revival and on Thursday night two very special things happened. First, a forty-eight-year-old man came to the altar and got born again.

Second, a lady of about the same age also came to the altar and knelt and prayed with the pastor's wife for a good long time. She got up from that altar and said, "I was planning on going home tonight and taking pills and ending my life. I just couldn't see any reason to live. I came to the meeting tonight, I heard what I needed to hear, and I came and got right with God. Now I don't want to die; now I do have a reason to live!"

I am so glad I got to be part of that. But I am also glad that a man with some resources, a man who could have bought $20,000 worth of toys or electronics, instead, chose to buy a tent so churches can have meetings just like that one, and so I could preach and so that man could get saved, and that lady could have her life saved.

What are you going to do with what you have?

Chapter Fifteen
Squeezing It In And Wrapping It Up

James 5:9 *Grudge not one against another, brethren, lest ye be condemned: behold, the judge standeth before the door.* **10** *Take, my brethren, the prophets, who have spoken in the name of the Lord, for an example of suffering affliction, and of patience.* **11** *Behold, we count them happy which endure. Ye have heard of the patience of Job, and have seen the end of the Lord; that the Lord is very pitiful, and of tender mercy.* **12** *But above all things, my brethren, swear not, neither by heaven, neither by the earth, neither by any other oath: but let your yea be yea; and your nay, nay; lest ye fall into condemnation.* **13** *Is any among you afflicted? let him pray. Is any merry? let him sing psalms.* **14** *Is any sick among you? let him call for the elders of the church; and let them pray over him, anointing him with oil in the name of the Lord:* **15** *And the prayer of faith shall save the sick, and the Lord shall raise him up; and if he have committed sins, they shall be forgiven him.* **16** *Confess your faults one to another, and pray one for another, that ye may be healed. The effectual fervent prayer of a righteous man availeth much.* **17** *Elias was a man subject to like passions as we are, and he prayed earnestly that it might not rain: and it rained not on the earth by the space of three years and six months.* **18** *And he prayed again, and the heaven gave rain, and the earth brought forth her fruit.* **19** *Brethren, if any of you do err from the truth, and one convert him;* **20** *Let him know, that he which converteth* *the sinner from the error of his way shall save a soul from death, and shall hide a multitude of sins.*

As we often see in the writings of the other New Testament authors, especially the apostle Paul, as James brings his letter to a close, he is going to pack a great deal of instruction in just a few short verses.

A warning about attitude

James 5:9 *Grudge not one against another, brethren, lest ye be condemned: behold, the judge standeth before the door.*

Grudge is from the word *stenadzo*. It means to groan, sigh, grumble, complain, find fault, be in ill humor. What a word! James was telling the believers to whom he was writing, church people, not to grumble and complain against each other.

Either James had a time machine and was prone to secretly visit the churches of our day, or churches have changed very little from his day to ours. How interesting and befuddling is it to realize that the first century church, the church made up of people who had heard Christ and/or the apostles themselves preach and teach, had the exact same sinful tendencies and "church issues" that our churches still have two thousand years removed from the time of Christ and the apostles.

How exactly does the spirit of grumbling come to be? Albert Barnes gave a classic take on this thought and passage:

"This may arise from many causes; either because others have advantages which we have not, and we are discontented and unhappy, as if it were wrong in them to have such enjoyments; or because we, without reason, suppose they intend to slight and neglect us; or because we are ready to take offence at any little thing, and to 'pick a quarrel' with them. There are some persons who are always grumbling. They have a sour, dissatisfied, discontented temper; they see no excellence in other persons; they are displeased that others are more prospered, honoured, and beloved than they are themselves;

they are always complaining of what others do, not because they are injured, but because others seem to them to be weak and foolish; they seem to feel that it becomes them to complain if everything is not done precisely as in their estimation it should be. It is needless to say that this spirit--the offspring of pride--will make any man lead a wretched life; and equally needless to say that it is wholly contrary to the spirit of the gospel."

I could sum that up in just a few words; some people are only happy when they are miserable.

In the early days of our church, we had a gentleman who was constantly getting this grudging, grumbling, complaining attitude about him. Time and time again he would come to different members of the church and say to them, "You tell preacher that I'm never coming back." To their credit, our people were always likely to respond the exact same way; "If you want him told that, you go tell him yourself!"

Finally, after a few years of this constantly sorry attitude, I had just about had my limit. And it was during one of those times where I had exactly one nerve left that he called bright and early on Monday morning. I picked up the phone and pleasantly said, "Hello!" And the very next thing I heard was his sour voice saying, "I want you to know, I am not happy."

I blew a gasket. Before I could even stop and think I shouted into the phone, "When have you ever not been unhappy?!?"

The next thing I heard was a dial tone, and he never came back.

By the way, I do not regret that, not even a tiny little bit. My blood pressure has gone down forty points since that day.

Is there a result, a fruit that is produced by this type of grudging attitude that James spoke of? Yes, the text itself gives us the result. We find that being of this attitude will result in us being condemned:

James 5:9 *Grudge not one against another, brethren, lest ye be condemned: behold, the judge standeth before the door.*

There is a choice bit of irony in this verse that is normally missed entirely when people comment on it. James has been laying out a scenario where people are griping and complaining about each other. In other words, they believe that someone else is wrong and needs to be dealt with.

But James said that when we complain against each other, we ourselves are at risk of being condemned. He said that the Judge, God Himself, standeth before the door.

When a judge is standing before the door, it is an indication that he is about to enter the courtroom and deliver his sentence. So, follow the word picture here.

James is dealing with people who believe that others are in the wrong, and they are grudging against them, they are griping and complaining about them. They can never be happy, because "someone else is always a problem."

So, James takes that person into the courtroom, as if the case has already been laid out, and everyone is waiting for the judge to come in and give his sentence.

And finally, the judge does come in. He looks over at the person you have been griping and complaining about, the person you have been grudging over...and says nothing.

But then he looks over at you, the complainer, and says, "I find you guilty of grudging against your brother. I convict you for your hard-heartedness and non-charitable attitude towards your own brothers and sisters in Christ."

That certainly changes things, now doesn't it! When we realize that God expects us to be as gracious and merciful to others as He is to us, and when we realize that He will condemn us if we ever get to be constant complainers and murmurers about others, it will change those sour attitudes.

A witness from the past

James 5:10 *Take, my brethren, the prophets, who have spoken in the name of the Lord, for an example of suffering affliction, and of patience.*

It is one thing to tell people not to murmur and complain and gripe against each other, not to be at each other's throats. It is quite another thing to realize that what you are being asked is actually possible to do.

James knew something. He knew that people did not have to grudge and gripe and complain and murmur against each other. And the reason he knew this was because he remembered a group of people who proved it.

James quickly told his readers of whom he was thinking. He was thinking about the prophets. These people had lost everything, many of them had even been tortured in horrible ways before they were even allowed to die. And yet as you look back at the lives of the prophets, men who were thrown in prisons and dungeons and dark holes in the ground, men who were lied about, men who were stolen from, you do not find those prophets grudging against the people that were treating them in such horrible manners.

Moses was constantly badgered and harassed and lied about. And yet he offered to have his own name blotted out rather than to see the people left to die in the wilderness.

Jeremiah was falsely accused of treason, thrown into a mud pit to die, nearly starved to death, was constantly insulted, and yet he served the people as their prophet for more than sixty years.

The prophets, despite how they were treated, chose to love and be merciful. The point from James was, the people he was writing to were not being persecuted by their brethren, *they were just ill with each other*! If the prophets could be kind, so could they.

James 5:11 *Behold, we count them happy which endure. Ye have heard of the patience of Job, and have seen the end of the Lord; that the Lord is very pitiful, and of tender mercy.*

The subject matter has not changed. James is still dealing with people whom he is trying to convince not to grudge against each other. He is still dealing with people who are ill-tempered toward each other. He is dealing with people who think they have a reason to quit church, to leave the fellowship, but who really do not.

The church is often plagued by people who seem to think that quitting is the solution to making them happy. But according to what James said in this verse, quitting does not produce happiness, but enduring does. By way of example, he mentions the man Job. Please notice that he does so as if Job was a real live historical person because Job was, in fact, a real live historical person. James, who was two thousand years closer to Job than we are, regarded him as being a historical character.

For Job, things went very hard. But there is one part of what Job went through that specifically plays into what James is speaking of here. Job was blistered unjustly by his friends. Take a look at just a few examples of this:

Eliphaz:

Job 4:7 *Remember, I pray thee, who ever perished, being innocent? or where were the righteous cut off?*

Bildad:

Job 8:1 *Then answered Bildad the Shuhite, and said,* **2** *How long wilt thou speak these things? and how long shall the words of thy mouth be like a strong wind?* **3** *Doth God pervert judgment? or doth the Almighty pervert justice?* **4** *If thy children have sinned against him, and he have cast them away for their transgression;* **5** *If thou wouldest seek unto God betimes, and make thy supplication to the Almighty;* **6** *If thou wert pure and upright; surely now he would awake for thee...*

Zophar:

Job 11:3 *Should thy lies make men hold their peace? and when thou mockest, shall no man make thee ashamed?* **4** *For thou hast said, My doctrine is pure, and I am clean in thine eyes.* **5** *But oh that God would speak, and open his lips against thee;* **6** *And that he would shew thee the secrets of wisdom, that they are double to that which is!* ***Know therefore that God exacteth of thee less than thine iniquity deserveth.***

Eliphaz:

Job 22:5 *Is not thy wickedness great? and thine iniquities infinite? 6 For thou hast taken a pledge from thy brother for nought, and stripped the naked of their clothing. 7 Thou hast not given water to the weary to drink, and thou hast withholden bread from the hungry.*

I believe this is one of the main things James had in mind when he said what he said about Job. The context points that direction. James is still dealing with people who are ill-tempered toward each other. He is dealing with people who think they have a reason to quit church, to leave the fellowship, but who really do not. And in that context, he says in so many words, "If you think you have it bad trying to deal with each other, look at how bad Job had it. And yet, not only did he not quit, he actually turned around and prayed for the people who were giving him such a hard time."

I do not even know if I can muster up the appropriate level of sarcasm when I say, "Wow, what a concept! What a concept, that we who have been redeemed by the grace of God should be graceful and patient and merciful to each other, rather than grudging and griping and complaining and murmuring at each other."

What a concept indeed.

A word about your word

James 5:12 *But above all things, my brethren, swear not, neither by heaven, neither by the earth, neither by any other oath: but let your yea be yea; and your nay, nay; lest ye fall into condemnation.*

When James says, *above all things*, you know, number one, that this is a big deal, and number two, that this was a constant issue for them. So what did he mean by what he said?

Here is a passage that runs along the same lines:

Matthew 5:34 *But I say unto you, Swear not at all; neither by heaven; for it is God's throne: 35 Nor by the earth; for it is his footstool: neither by Jerusalem; for it is the city of the great King. 36 Neither shalt thou swear by thy head, because thou canst not make one hair white or black. 37 But let your* *communication be, Yea, yea; Nay, nay: for whatsoever is more than these cometh of evil.*

Clearly, what James and Jesus said raises some questions concerning some things that we do today. For instance, does all of this mean that we are not allowed to "testify under oath?" Many religious groups believe that this is exactly what these passages mean.

But this is not even remotely what James was seeing, thinking about, and railing against, nor was it what Christ had in mind. The Jews of James's day, from which most of the early converts to Christianity came, were legendary for being so untrustworthy that they had to swear with greater and greater oaths to be believed by anyone. One rabbi taught that "A man might swear with his lips and annul it in his heart; and then the oath was not binding." (Clarke, 6:826) Because of things like this, many people did not trust them, and so they would swear by their town, and then by their country, and then by the whole earth, and then by the universe.

Jesus and James both were telling them to be so honest that such "swearing" was not necessary. James was instructing them to be so trustworthy that if they said "yes" everyone believed it, and if they said "no" everyone believed it.

By the way, if you are a member of one of the religious sects that believe that swearing under oath to tell the truth is wrong, please understand that calling it another name (affirming, promising) does not change what it actually is. That makes as much sense as believing that eating pizza is a sin and yet thinking that eating round flat rolled out dough with tomato sauce and cheese and pepperoni on it is perfectly fine.

Be honest. If it is going to make you look good, tell the truth. If it is going to make you look bad, tell the truth. If it is going to make money for you, tell the truth. If it is going to cost you money, tell the truth. If your parents are going to love you for it, tell the truth. If your parents are going to ground you for eternity for it, tell the truth. Just tell the truth!

A way for you to go

James 5:13 *Is any among you afflicted? let him pray. Is any merry? let him sing psalms.* **14** *Is any sick among you? let him call for the elders of the church; and let them pray over him, anointing him with oil in the name of the Lord:* **15** *And the prayer of faith shall save the sick, and the Lord shall raise him up; and if he have committed sins, they shall be forgiven him.*

In these verses, James deals with three conditions that his readers might be in:

Afflicted:

James 5:13a *Is any among you afflicted? let him pray.*

Afflicted is from the word *kakopatheo*. It means to suffer hardships. That is pretty general, it could be most anything. Life tends to "afflict people," making them feel like they have a giant target on their back. People are often afflicted by poor health or by having an ogre for a boss or by having to deal with wayward children or by suffering from depression or anxiety or any of a thousand other possible things.

So, what did James tell people to do when they feel afflicted? He told them to pray.

Given the fact that almost everyone feels afflicted on a pretty regular basis, does there not seem to be a disconnect between that fact and the amount of time we spend praying? If God expects us to pray about our afflictions, and we day by day face afflictions all through the day, it would seem that those afflictions would serve to make us people consistent and powerful in prayer.

And yet what do we find as reality? My evaluation is that we are either not nearly as afflicted as we think, or we are far weaker in prayer than we should be.

Merry:

James 5:13b... *Is any merry? let him sing psalms.*

There is a proper way to behave when things are going poorly, and there is a proper way to behave when things are going well! Celebrating with a few brews is not it. Singing psalms is.

A psalm was and is a believer's song, done primarily on stringed instruments. Many of them were joyful and uplifting,

167

and they are perfect choices in times when our hearts are light and merry. Psalms glorified God and encouraged God's people.

This is not just "the Psalms" being spoken of. James did not say, "Sing one of the Psalms." Those type of songs were being written even in his day hundreds of years after the book of Psalms had been completed. There are still songs being written in our day that fit the template that James was describing.

If God has been good to you and you are having a good day and your heart is merry and light, do not bottle that up; sing about it! Make others happy along with you.

Sick:

James 5:14 *Is any sick among you? let him call for the elders of the church; and let them pray over him, anointing him with oil in the name of the Lord:* **15** *And the prayer of faith shall save the sick, and the Lord shall raise him up; and if he have committed sins, they shall be forgiven him.*

And now we arrive at two verses with the power of dynamite wrapped up in them. There is so much here to see.

Look at the very first phrase: *Is any sick among you?*

Right off the bat, that one simple five-word phrase begins to shine the light on a fairly frustrating yet all too common doctrinal heresy. I am speaking of the weird notion that it is never God's will for any of His children to be sick and that if they just had enough faith, they never would get sick.

People actually believe that. And yet right here James referenced the fact that there were very likely some sick people among them.

The great apostle Paul himself knew a little bit about that:

2 Corinthians 12:7 *And lest I should be exalted above measure through the abundance of the revelations, there was given to me a thorn in the flesh, the messenger of Satan to buffet me, lest I should be exalted above measure.* **8** *For this thing I besought the Lord thrice, that it might depart from me.* **9** *And he said unto me, My grace is sufficient for thee: for my strength is made perfect in weakness. Most gladly therefore will I rather glory in my infirmities, that the power of Christ may rest upon me.*

Paul had an infirmity of the flesh. And far from being a sign that he did not have any faith and was somehow out of God's will, this passage tells us that it was actually God's express will that he had that infirmity of the flesh.

James knew that people were going to get sick. And in the particular situation they were in, he had some guidance for them when they did:

James 5:14 *Is any sick among you? let him call for the elders of the church; and let them pray over him, anointing him with oil in the name of the Lord:*

This instruction that James gave to them raises an interesting question; was there and is there something wrong or sinful about using the services of a doctor or other medical professional?

Certainly not. If you believe that God disapproves of doctors, you might want to try to explain why He had a doctor write two books of the New Testament! Both the book of Luke and the book of Acts were written by Luke, who was a medical doctor, and who, by the way, accompanied the apostle Paul on some of his missionary journeys. And far from Paul expressing displeasure over Luke being a doctor, he expressed in Scripture that he himself benefited from Luke being a doctor. Look what he called him:

Colossians 4:14 *Luke, the beloved physician,*

As many times as Paul was beaten and stoned and shipwrecked and abused, having a doctor alongside was a help.

James, who gave the instructions concerning sick people, never did rip into doctors or medicines. He spoke positively of prayer and anointing, but he did not ever speak negatively of doctoring or medicines.

Here was the situation. James, as he pointed out very early on in this epistle, was dealing with people who were going through some incredible hardships:

James 1:1 *James, a servant of God and of the Lord Jesus Christ, to the twelve tribes which are scattered abroad, greeting.* **2** *My brethren, count it all joy when ye fall into divers temptations;* **3** *Knowing this, that the trying of your faith worketh patience.*

169

These people to whom he was writing were scattered abroad because of the persecution that Christians were undergoing. They did not have the luxury, as we do, of simply strolling into the local doctor's office. But the very good God of heaven had a way for them to get help anyway:

James 5:14 *Is any sick among you? let him call for the elders of the church; and let them pray over him, anointing him with oil in the name of the Lord:* **15a** *And the prayer of faith shall save the sick, and the Lord shall raise him up...*

Let us go to the middle part of all of this first and deal with it, namely the anointing with oil. There are a couple of things I want you to understand. First of all, we still do this, we still anoint people with oil. But when we do, it is not quite the same as what they were doing and why. There is nothing wrong or sinful about the way we do it, please do not think that. But when they were anointing with oil, they were doing this particular part for medicinal reasons, not spiritual reasons.

Here is what Adam Clarke said:

"What is here recommended was to be done as a natural means of restoring health, which, while they used prayer and supplication to God, they were not to neglect. Oil in Judea was celebrated for its sanative qualities; so that they scarcely ever took a journey without carrying oil with them, (see in the case of the Samaritan,) with which they anointed their bodies, healed their wounds, bruises, &c. oil was and is frequently used in the east as a means of cure in very dangerous diseases; and in Egypt it is often used in the cure of the plague. Even in Europe it has been tried with great success in the cure of dropsy. And pure olive oil is excellent for recent wounds and bruises." (6:827)

In other words, these people who could not get to doctors were being doctored as well as they could be by people right there in the church. Clarke mentioned the case of the Good Samaritan, and he is right. The Good Samaritan used oil and wine in the wounds to help heal the man who had been left for

170

dead. That is what James was thinking of as well when he spoke of anointing with oil.

But the prayer of faith most certainly was and is a spiritual aspect. Neither one is to be neglected. If you or a loved one gets sick, pursue a cure both medicinally and spiritually.

Let me say it this way; we do not believe in modern so-called faith healers, but we absolutely believe in a God that can still heal. Look again what James said:

James 5:14 *Is any sick among you? let him call for the elders of the church; and let them pray over him, anointing him with oil in the name of the Lord:* **15a** ***And the prayer of faith shall save the sick, and the Lord shall raise him up...***

God can still heal, and we should still pray for it. But let me ask another question before we look at another part of this passage. Here is the question. Is verse fifteen to be regarded as an "always thing?" In other words, will the prayer of faith always save the sick? Will God always raise people up when we pray for them?

If that is what this verse means, then no one would ever even die! If that is what this verse means, Hebrews 9:27 would never be true:

Hebrews 9:27 *And as it is appointed unto men once to die, but after this the judgment:*

It is both inconsistent with the whole of Scripture and even with logic itself to believe that this passage means that if we just have enough faith to pray for people they will always be healed of their sickness.

What James is giving us, just like so many other promises of Scripture, has to fit under the umbrella of God's will. By that I mean if someone is sick and we pray for them, we should absolutely have faith that unless it is God's will to take them or unless, as in the case of the apostle Paul, God has a greater purpose for the sickness, He is going to do what James said here, He is going to heal them; He is going to raise them up.

We knelt before the altar in our church and anointed a lady with oil and prayed over her when the doctor said she was not going to make it. God healed her, and she was with us for a great many more years.

But the last time around no anointing and no prayer was going to change the fact that God was ready for her to come home.

God can heal, but God does not always heal.

But now let's look at another aspect of this verse. Here is the passage again:

James 5:14 *Is any sick among you? let him call for the elders of the church; and let them pray over him, anointing him with oil in the name of the Lord:* **15a** *And the prayer of faith shall save the sick, and the Lord shall raise him up...*

Look at the words of those two verses very carefully. Now please answer a question for me; who is it that needs to have "enough faith" for the healing to take place?

Not the sick person: the people praying over him!

When you watch moneygrubbing charlatans like Benny Hinn and other so-called faith healers of our day, you will find that they have given themselves the most amazing "out" for when someone does not get healed. No matter what the ailment is, if the person does not get healed, they will tell that person "You simply did not have enough faith. If you had just had more faith, I could have healed you."

No, that is not what James taught. According to what James said here, it would be much more accurate for the person who is not healed to look up at him and say, "You just simply did not have enough faith. If you had just had more faith, you could have healed me!"

Now look at the last part of verse fifteen:

James 5:15 *And the prayer of faith shall save the sick, and the Lord shall raise him up;* ***and if he have committed sins, they shall be forgiven him.***

The first part of this verse talks about a person being sick and needing healing, and the second part of this verse mentions that person who was sick and says that if he has committed sins, they shall be forgiven him. Does it sound sort of like James is saying that it is possible for a person's sickness to be caused by sin? Well, look at the next verse:

James 5:16 *Confess your faults one to another, and pray one for another, that ye may be healed. The effectual fervent prayer of a righteous man availeth much.*

Yes, that is exactly what James was saying. No, not all sickness is caused by sin. But yes, some sickness is, in fact, caused by sin. James knew that some of the church folks that were going to be coming to the elders for prayer and healing were experiencing sickness in their body either because of God's chastisement on them because of their sin or because of the natural consequences of the law of sowing and reaping in their life because of their sin. So, he was telling the elders to deal both with the physical aspects of the sickness and with any spiritual aspect of it as well.

By the way, it is in that context alone that the Bible tells us to *confess our faults one to another.* In other words, James is not telling us just to randomly blurt out our sin problem. He is saying that, especially when a person knows that their sin has caused the sickness, they need to be honest about that if they expect any help from God.

Yes, that part about the effectual fervent prayer of a righteous man availing much can be applied in pretty much every situation. But the immediate context in which James spoke it dealt with us praying for one another over the sin in our lives that is causing the damage in our lives.

A wonderful power

James 5:17 *Elias was a man subject to like passions as we are, and he prayed earnestly that it might not rain: and it rained not on the earth by the space of three years and six months.* **18** *And he prayed again, and the heaven gave rain, and the earth brought forth her fruit.*

James had just spoken of the effectual, fervent prayer of a righteous man and how powerful it was. Now he turns and gives an illustration of that. He harkens back to the Old Testament, and to the great prophet Elijah. He pointed out that Elijah was not a Superman. Elijah was a human being just like all the rest of us. And yet, when Elijah prayed earnestly, he was able to stop the rain for three and one-half years, and then pray and have the faucets of heaven open again.

Whether it is over sickness, or over sin, over a wayward child, over a home in trouble, over a nation in need of revival, we greatly underestimate the awesome power of prayer. We spend our time scheming and planning and thinking and doing and working, and those things are not necessarily bad. But without prayer, they may as well be the body of the vehicle with no engine. The power is not in our efforts; the power is in the God that we are praying to, and therefore it is the prayer that brings the power, not our efforts.

A watching for one another

James 5:19 *Brethren, if any of you do err from the truth, and one convert him;* **20** *Let him know, that he which converteth the sinner from the error of his way shall save a soul from death, and shall hide a multitude of sins.*

I have been pointing out for the duration of this book that James was a very strict and straight-laced individual. But I hope you have gotten the sense over these last several verses that he also deeply loved the people to whom he was writing. James wanted the best for them. Just like a pastor wants the best for his church members, James wanted the best for these Christians in the church of the first century.

In verse nineteen, he was still speaking to Christians, brethren. He mentioned that it would be possible for one of those Christians, one of those brethren, to err from the truth. The fact that you and I have gotten saved does not always mean that we will always be right or even that we will always be right with God.

So, when James spoke of the sinner being converted, he was not speaking of it the way we normally think of it when we hear those terms. He was not talking about a lost man; he was talking about a saved man. He was pointing out that sometimes we need to, "save the saved." Not from hell; that has already been dealt with. James here specifically spoke of saving them from death.

174

Do you remember what John the Apostle said that sounds similar?

1 John 5:16 *If any man see his brother sin a sin which is not unto death, he shall ask, and he shall give him life for them that sin not unto death. There is a sin unto death: I do not say that he shall pray for it.*

John and James were talking about the exact same thing. Christian, if you get out of sorts with God, and it goes on long enough, and it gets to be a big enough problem, it can become the sin unto death. In other words, God will actually take your life rather than have you continue to live and do damage to His name.

No wonder James and John both referenced praying for a brother who is going bad.

Notice the last thing that James said:

James 5:20 *Let him know, that he which converteth the sinner from the error of his way shall save a soul from death,* ***and shall hide a multitude of sins.***

When we think of "hiding sins," we normally think of that in the negative sense, especially since Proverbs 28:13 specifically commanded us never to try to cover our sins. But in the sense that James is using it, it is right, and even biblical:

Proverbs 10:12 *Hatred stirreth up strifes: but love covereth all sins.*

How does it cover them in this case? By getting them to stop and getting that which they have already done forgiven. This is our responsibility one to another. Why do you think James told them to confess their faults? That is an excellent way to get people to stop them.

Now look at that verse one more time; I want to show you one last thing as we bring our study of the book of James to a close.

James 5:20 *Let him know, that he which converteth the sinner from the error of his way shall save a soul from death, and shall hide a multitude of sins.*

Get that verse, the very last verse of the book of James, in your mind.

Now let me show you how several other New Testament books close.

Romans 16:27 *To God only wise, be glory through Jesus Christ for ever. Amen.*

1 Corinthians 16:24 *My love be with you all in Christ Jesus. Amen.*

2 Corinthians 13:14 *The grace of the Lord Jesus Christ, and the love of God, and the communion of the Holy Ghost, be with you all. Amen.*

Galatians 6:18 *Brethren, the grace of our Lord Jesus Christ be with your spirit. Amen.*

I could give you many more examples like these. These and other New Testament books end very positively and very flowingly. Now look once again at the last verse of the book of James.

James 5:20 *Let him know, that he which converteth the sinner from the error of his way shall save a soul from death, and shall hide a multitude of sins.*

That is not a "well wish" of an ending; it is a warning. It is not flowing; it is incredibly abrupt. It is not mean or harsh, but it is intense and even potentially ominous.

In other words, James is ending this book the exact same way he has written this book. He is still holding that perfectly straight plumb line, still demanding that everyone evaluate themselves by it, and still pointing out the consequences of not doing so.

So, I have a question that will allow me to apply the entirety of this book to us as we end our study. This man, James, demanded such holy living and was so unbending in what Scripture says and what God expects that he would absolutely be called a legalist in our day. Mind you, people calling him that, just as people who call people like James today legalists, have no idea what legalism actually was. But that will not stop the accusations.

So here is my question. Did James just demand all of this of us, or did he also demand it of himself? Was he genuine, or was he merely a self-righteous hypocrite?

The world, and even much of the church, would love to find out that he was a hypocrite, because that would, in their minds, let them off the hook for everything James demanded.

But what does history tell us about James, the man who wrote this ultra-straight, razor-sharp book?

The International Bible Encyclopedia says,

> "The Jews respected him, and the Christians revered him. No man among them commanded the esteem of the entire population as much as he.

> "Josephus (Ant., XX, ix) tells us that Ananus the high priest had James stoned to death and that the most equitable of the citizens immediately rose in revolt against such a lawless procedure, and Ananus was deposed after only three months' rule. This testimony of Josephus simply substantiates all that we know from other sources concerning the high standing of James in the whole community." (3:1563)

In other words, James lived what he wrote; James lived what he preached. And if he can live it then, in those awful days of persecution and apathy, we can most assuredly live it now.

Works Cited

Barnes, Albert. <u>Notes, Explanatory and Practical: on the</u>
<u>General Epistles of James, Peter, John and June</u>. New
<u>York:</u> Haper & Brother, 1852

Bible.org. https://bible.org/illustration/i-wish-you-were-my-
little-girl

Clarke, Adam. <u>Clarke's Commentary</u>. 6 vols. New York:
Abingdon-Cokesbury Press

CNN.com (https://www.cnn.com/2017/05/02/us/michael-
slager-federal-plea/index.html)

Daily Walk Devotion, July 10, 1993

FoxNews.com
(http://www.foxnews.com/us/2018/01/25/preacher-
who-cheated-using-ashley-madison-tried-hivring-hit-
man-on-dark-web-in-bid-to-murder-wife-cops-
say.html)

ISBE, <u>International Standard Bible Encyclopaedia.</u> Grand
Rapids: Eerdmans, MI, 1955.

LATimes.com
http://articles.latimes.com/2004/oct/04/opinion/oe-
ehrenfeld4. June 9, 2018

Lucado, Max, <u>In the Eye of the Storm</u>, Word Publishing, 1991

Luther, Martin.
https://www.defendingthebride.com/bb/deuterocanonic

al5.html. Preface to the Epistle of St. James, German Translation of Bible, 1522 (Accessed December 2018)

Opensocietyfoundations.org (https://www.opensocietyfoundations.org/people/george-soros June 9, 2018)

People's New Testament Commentary. Power Bible CD, 2003

Sermonillustrations.com. http://www.sermonillustrations.com/a-z/t/temptation.htm

Spurgeon, Charles. Lectures to My Student., Grand Rapids: Zondervan. 1954

Today in the Word, Moody Bible Institute, January 1992.

USA Magazine, in the Shelby Star of January 14, 2007:

WPDE.com (http://wpde.com/news/local /timmonsville-naacp-president-says-was-racially-profiled-body-cam-video-shows-otherwise) May 22, 2018

www.ingramcontent.com/pod-product-compliance
Lightning Source LLC
Chambersburg PA
CBHW072005040426
42447CB00009B/1494